20 Walks

in Hastings and the
1066 countryside

**A Further Publication by
Hastings Rambling Club**

Previous Publications:
Rambles in Hastings and Rother – 1975
Revised edition – 1980
20 Walks in and around Hastings – 1989
Favourite Walks in the Hastings Area – 1996

ISBN 0 9514932 2 1

Printed and bound by Berfort Limited
Hastings, East Sussex (01424) 722733 • Email office@berfort.co.uk

Front Cover photograph:
Brede Level
Back Cover photograph:
Approaching Caldbec Hill, Battle

20 Walks
in Hastings and
the 1066 countryside

A Further Publication by
Hastings Rambling Club

Preface

The committee of the Hastings Rambling Club would like
to record its gratitude to all those who have contributed in a
variety of ways to the publication of this book and especially
to Iris Lockwood, a member of the book committee, who
sadly passed away prior to publication.

The overall design of this book, photographs (unless
credited), maps and illustrations are the work of
Christopher O'Brien.

The maps are based on the Ordnance Survey maps
with the sanction of the Controller of H.M.Stationery Office.
Crown Copyright reserved.

All walkers are asked to observe the Country Code
given below.

Be safe – plan ahead and follow any signs. Leave gates
and property as you find them. Protect plants and animals,
and take your litter home. Keep dogs under close control.
Consider other people.

Where, for a short distance, the route of the ramble follows or
crosses a busy highway with fast moving traffic it is essential
to proceed with great care.

Contents

Key to Map Symbols

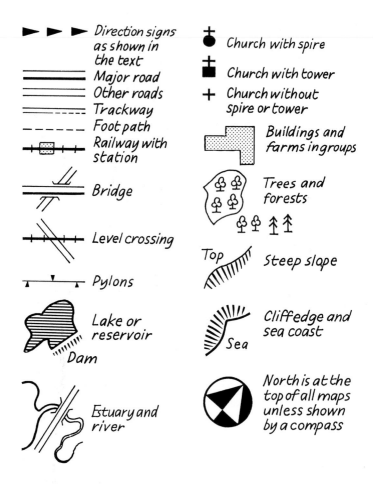

► ► ► Direction signs as shown in the text

⚊⚊⚊ Major road

⚊⚊⚊ Other roads

⚊⚊- - - Trackway

- - - - - Foot path

Railway with station

Bridge

Level crossing

Pylons

Lake or reservoir
Dam

Estuary and river

☥ Church with spire

☩ Church with tower

✝ Church without spire or tower

Buildings and farms in groups

Trees and forests

Top Steep slope

Cliff edge and sea coast
Sea

North is at the top of all maps unless shown by a compass

On the maps the numbers enclosed in circles correspond with the bracketed numbers in the text.

4

Introduction

Our last publication in 1996 contained twenty of what we considered to be the best walks in our area. Our new booklet, which we have called "20 Walks in Hastings and the 1066 Countryside" covers a similar area but this time we have included a good number of new walks.

As before they are of varying lengths, from three to eight miles and cover the stretch of countryside from Rye in the east, to Bodiam in the north and Stonegate and Burwash in the north-west. Most of this is in the High Weald Area of Outstanding Natural Beauty. We have tried to include and indicate features of interest as well as areas which are of great natural beauty.

The villages and small towns from which several walks start are in themselves attractive and worth a visit for their historical or architectural interest. They are linked to agriculture, forestry and to the old iron industry. Several walks in the book use paths and tracks which served the old iron industry sites. Now covered by many years' growth of vegetation it is easy to imagine them as deep rutted muddy tracks when the iron products were being transported along them to their destination.

Other paths link farms to villages and outlying hamlets to major routes. Although their original purpose may often have disappeared they have been preserved and now are an amenity which all can enjoy.

Legislation has helped to ensure that rights of way are maintained in reasonable condition. As far as possible we have tried to avoid routes which present difficulties. However, there may be situations where care is needed because of a dilapidated stile or the way is unclear owing to the quick growth of summer vegetation.

All the walks described follow rights of way as shown on the current Ordnance Survey "Explorer" maps and it would be helpful to have the appropriate map when following a route.

The walk descriptions are accurate at the time of going to print (2005) but changes, usually minor, may occure at a later date.

Stout shoes will suffice for summer walking but leather boots or wellingtons are recommended for the winter. After heavy rain Wealden clay can become very sticky.

This book, like previous publications, has been compiled by members of Hastings Rambling Club. Most of the walks are ones which have been enjoyed by club members over the years and we hope you will enjoy them in the same way.

Squeeze Gate, near Burwash

Walk No. 1

A walk around the Old Town of Hastings
1¾ miles (2.25 kilometres)

The Stade, Hastings Old Town

Although this walk actually starts from the West Hill of Hastings, if one is arriving in the town by train it is possible to walk from the station, through the town centre and up on to the hill in approx. 20 minutes.

Emerging from the station, walk down Station Approach to the traffic lights and continue ahead, over the cross-roads, down Havelock road to the Town Centre. Walk along Wellington Place, with the York Buildings on the left (the broad pedestrian precinct) and turn left before the under-pass and cross Albert road to enter Wellington Square. The author, Lewis Carroll (1832-1898) was a frequent visitor to the square, staying at No. 2.

Follow one of the diagonal paths to the top right-hand corner and continue up a flight of steps into Castlehill road and turn left up the road. At the brow, cross the road and proceed up the pathway, called Wallingers Walk, alongside a garden (which was formerly a graveyard for St Mary-in-the-Castle Church). Continue climbing, then cross the road and up some more steps, leading to the West Hill. Continue past the children's play-ground and before you cross Plynlimmon road it is worth turning around and looking at the view of the town and Beachy Head in the distance. Continue up the pavement until Alpine road is reached, keeping the houses on the left and the green on the right.

(1) To start the walk take the diagonal path, almost opposite Alpine road, near the phone-box,

Walk No. 1

towards a lamp-post at the junction of the two paths, continue straight ahead towards a flight of concrete steps. The path to the left of these steps goes along to the caves. Descend these steps then turn left down some more steps, under the extension of Harpsichord House and continue following the steps down and round the corner into

Coburg Place, passing some tall Victorian buildings on the left. At the bottom of Coburg Place, **(2)** opposite St.Clements Church, (dating from approx. 1380) the Hastings Borough Church, turn left along Croft Road, past the Old Church House and other fine houses and noting No. 23 "Edwards Rest for Freemasons". Follow the road

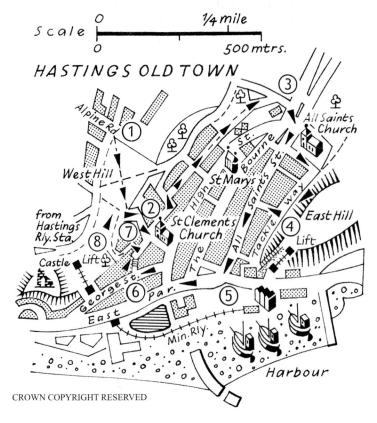

Scale

0   ¼ mile

0   500 mtrs.

HASTINGS OLD TOWN

round the corner and then turn right along the Croft, noting the tall Georgian houses on the left and further along on the right a house faced with glazed bricks. The end of this unadopted road leads into a passageway, known as Salters Lane, bear slightly right here and turn left into Love Lane. Continue along this lane, past the boundary walls of several houses and when the path begins to ascend the hill take the gravel path on the right, opposite a lamp-post. Continue along this path and at the next lamp-post pause to look back along the valley of the Old Town - here can be seen the three churches of All Saints, St.Mary-Star-Of-the Sea and St.Clements. Further on the path goes alongside a long red-brick wall and at the end of the path turn right down to the main road.

(3) Turn right and cross on the pedestrian-crossing then right along the pavement, passing the "Hastings Old Town" sign and continuing until turning left up a short path, past the stone Celtic Market Cross into Harold Road. Cross the road towards "The Old Rectory" and turn right and then left up through All Saints Churchyard, keeping the church on the left, towards the lych gate.

Go through this and turn right down Tackleway, with its varied architecture. Approx. 50 yards (46 metres) from the lych gate, note the

brick building which is the back of the Ebenezer Particular Baptist Chapel (built in 1817) but now a private dwelling. Continue down the road and a short distance past Strawberry Cottage turn right down (4) Woods Passage and follow it as it twists and turns down to All Saints Street. At the end it goes underneath one of the old houses and these passages are known as "Cat creeps"

On emerging into All Saints Street, note the 15 th. Century house almost opposite, reputed to be the residence of the mother of Sir Cloudesley Shovell. Turn left down the street, past some interesting old houses and on the right the Cinque Port Arms, dating from 1824 but rebuilt after a fire in 1925. It stands on part of the site of a Tudor inn called "The Chequers". Further down on the left side see the unusual cottage called "The Piece of Cheese", built in 1871 as a workshop. Observe the amusing plaque about Mr and Mrs Michael Mouse.

(5) At the end of the street is Winkle Island, go across the road to the pavement opposite, noting the black net huts to the left, then turn right past the amusement arcade to the pedestrian crossing, cross this and enter the High Street. Then take the second turning on the left into George Street and continue until you reach "The

Walk No. 1

Pump House". **(6)** Climb the steps alongside the "Pub" and continue up to Hill Street. At the top of the steps is the Old Lantern House, used in the days of the Smugglers. A short distance along turn left up Exmouth Place but before doing so, note ahead the house called "The Kicking Donkey" which was formerly a pub, and another view of St.Clements Church. At the top of Exmouth Place, on the right, see the plaque on the wall of West Hill House recording that Kate McMullen (Dame Catherine Cookson) lived there from 1931-33. **(7)** Turning left along the road there is also a plaque on the wall of Rock House, stating that Dr. Elizabeth Blackwell lived and worked there for thirty years until she died in 1910. She qualified as a doctor in America and was the first woman to be placed on the British Medical Register in 1859. **(8)** Just past this house, go through the opening ahead then turn right and climb up the grassy slope on to the West Hill and back to the start of the walk.

St. Clements Church, Hastings

Walk No. 2

Ecclesbourne and Fairlight Glens
4 miles (6.4 kilometres)

Fairlight Glen   Photo: Brian Doble

This walk gives an introduction to Hastings Country Park which is part of the High Weald Area of Outstanding Natural Beauty. The Park extends from Hastings to Fairlight and comprises three glens, Ecclesbourne, Fairlight and Warren, the first two of which are included in the walk. The route is quite hilly and can be muddy in winter.

The walk starts from the car park off Barley Lane, next to Shearbarn Caravan Park and can be reached

from the Old Town which is at the eastern end of Hastings.

Leave the car park by the main entrance and turn right along the lane passing by the side of the locked metal gate which stops access to motor vehicles. Ignore paths to the left and right.

You are now on the route of the 1066 Hastings Walk and Cycle Way. After about 500 yards (450 metres) turn right down a track by

Walk No. 2

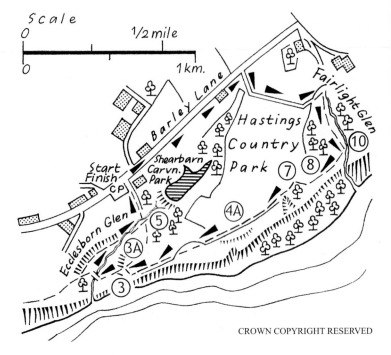

a metal post. Go along the track between fields to a stile and gate and continue with a hedge on the left towards Fairlight Glen.

After a while the track bends sharply left and skirts the edge of a wood. Pass the notice announcing "Fairlight Glen" and at the next junction turn sharp right to follow the arrow indicating "Fairlight Glen" and "Ecclesbourne Glen".

Fairlight Glen is thickly wooded and contains plants which are

nationally important . It is also a good site for birdwatching.

The broad path descends gradually towards the sea. At marker post **no.10** change direction and turn to the right to follow the arrow to Ecclesbourne Glen. This path is quite steep and you may wish to use the strategically placed benches to rest and enable you to admire the view of the cliffs and beach below.

Continue up the steps at post **no.8** and follow the path to Ecclesbourne

Walk No. 2

Glen. The path continues through the wood and at post **no.7** you should bear left to take the path to Ecclesbourne Glen Lower. Continue along the top of the cliff with a fence and gorse and blackberry bushes on your left. At post **no. 4A** carry on along the cliff and then go downhill and through a wide gap in a fence to a bench giving a good view of Hastings and the Harbour Arm, and also Beachy Head if the day is clear.

You are now looking down on the end of Ecclesbourne Glen. Turn right, then shortly left through bushes and down steps to the bottom of the glen. Pass post **no.3** and carry on up the steps marked "To East Hill", and look out for a path to the right by a bench about halfway up the hill. Take this

path which will lead you through Ecclesbourne Glen .

The Glen is a steep river valley composed of eroded clay and sandstone. It is heavily wooded, giving it an almost sub-tropical atmosphere. It is a site of special scientific interest. Follow the path past interesting sandstone outcrops on your left and continue downhill with a stream and small cascades on your right. Carry on across the footbridge, ignoring a bridge and path to the right at post **no. 3A** and go up steps to the end of the wood. Turn left along the grassy track to reach a junction of paths and post **no.5**. Take the indicated path which ascends the hill and leads to the edge of the Caravan Park and on to the Car Park.

Walk No. 3

Pett Circular *5 miles (8 kilometres)*

Pett is a delightful village about five miles (8 kilometres) east of Hastings with pubs that serve good food. Parking is available in the village in a lay-by opposite the Methodist Church which is just past the village hall.

(1) Take the footpath opposite the Two Sawyers. Walk down through Roughter's Wood on a well-established footpath. When you leave the wood walk towards the road by the farmhouse through two fields along a fenced pathway.

(2) Cross the road and go over the stile. Continue walking beside the hedge on your right through the next two fields to the next road by Winterstow Farm Cottages. Cross over Peter James Lane and continue across the next field to the junction of five footpaths. Do not go over

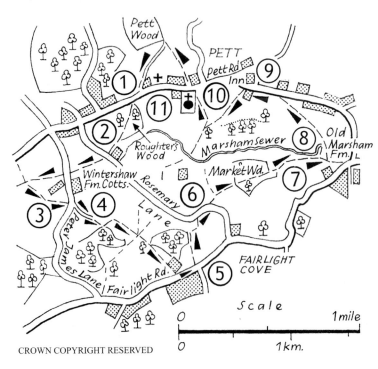

CROWN COPYRIGHT RESERVED

Walk No. 3

the stile in the hedge. Turn left and follow the footpath along the hedge to a bridge over a stream next to Cherry Garden Farm. Cross the farm track and go through the gate. There is a junction of two footpaths, take the footpath to the left.

(3) Walk diagonally left across the field up to a stile in the far corner and cross Peter James Lane to a drive leading to a house. Walk along the drive to the house and follow the footpath that goes along the side of the garden. Go through the gate at the back of the house and over a stile into a field. Follow the hedge on the right. Where the hedge bends right go ahead to the stile in the hedge opposite.

(4) Follow the footpath through the next field veering slightly to the left. Go over the stile at the end and continue walking along the hedge on your right to a stile where there is a junction of five footpaths. Go over the stile and follow the footpath to your left towards a gap in the hedge. Go through this gap and walk towards a house in the top right-hand corner of the field (you will be able to see its chimney). Go over a stile and walk along the track alongside the house; go through a gate and out to the main road. Turn left at the main road and walk until you come to a garage and post-office within 220 yards (200 metres) where you will find a footpath on the left.

(5) Follow the footpath through a gap in the hedge and go over a bridge. Go alongside the left hand newly-established hedge to the mature hedge ahead. You will notice an orchard on your left that was planted in Spring 2004 and has many rare varieties of English apples and other fruits. Continue through the hedge where there is a bridge and stile. The footpath goes around the edge of the next field. Continuing in the same direction go over two stiles, a bridge and along the left-hand side of a garden of a house to Rosemary Lane.

(6) Go over the stile and turn right. Walk along the road for a distance of 220 yards (200 metres) and take the second footpath to the left by a garage. Walk diagonally right up the hill to a stile in the right hand corner of the field. Continue in the same direction across the next field to Market Wood keeping fairly close to the right-hand hedge. Walk through the wood along the path, which is at times indistinct, to a stile beside a field-gate. In Springtime the wood is covered with bluebells. Walk across the large field going slightly to your left towards the bottom left-hand corner where there is a gate, track and stream.

(7) There are several footpaths around Old Marsham Farm. Your route is along the concrete track to the hedge by the house. After about

110 yards (100 metres) turn sharp left at the hedge and follow round the edge of the field by a small stream to a bridge. Cross this bridge and note the sign on the bridge indicating that Hastings Rambling Club constructed it in 1988.

(8) Walk up the slope towards the hedge at the top left-hand corner of the field and cross over a stile. Continue in the same direction to a fence. As you walk up this field you will see the brick remains of a radar tower built in the 1939-45 war in the next field. Cross a stile in this fence, keeping the radar tower to your left, and go towards the top left-hand corner of the field. Cross the stile and turn left into Pett road.

(9) Walk towards the village of Pett until you see a bus shelter on your left almost opposite the Royal Oak. Cross the stile by the shelter and walk across the playing field towards another stile by the tennis court. There are some benches in the field if you want to rest. Continue, bearing slightly to the left, through two fields down the hill towards some trees and a pond in the bottom right-hand corner. At the junction of footpaths, by a large stone, turn right and walk back up the field towards Pett. Walk along the hedge through three fields and stiles towards the parish church of St Mary and St Peter. The church spire was used as a navigational aid by sailors coming into port in the past. When you get to the main road turn left and walk 30 yards (27 metres) towards a footpath on your right. You will note an interesting V-shaped gap in the churchyard's brick wall as you walk along the road.

(10) Take the path on the right and walk along the boundary of a garden. Walk diagonally across the next field towards Pett Wood. At the edge of Pett Wood you come to a junction of two footpaths. Turn left and go over a stile 20 yards (18 metres) away. Continue in the same direction passing a pond on your left. There is a large garden ahead of you, do not go through the gate! Follow the footpath along the left-hand boundary of the garden towards a track. Cross a stile and turn left and walk along the track until you come to the main road.

(11) Turn left and you will see the lay-by opposite the Methodist chapel.

Walk No. 4

Pett Level and Winchelsea Circular
5 miles (8 kilometres)

This is an easy walk which can be extended by exploring the ancient town and Cinque Port of Winchelsea. The new town of Winchelsea was built on a hill after the old town was swept away in a storm in October 1250 and it is set out in a grid pattern. There is much

St. Thomas's Church, Winchelsea

Walk No. 4

of interest in the town. The church of St. Thomas is well worth a visit, as is the small museum. The town itself is a delight to walk around with its well-kept houses and colourful gardens.

The walk starts on the Pett Level road, map reference TQ908152, where there is a finger post and stile. The first part of the walk is across Pett Level, an area of marshland used for grazing sheep. This area, together with the foreshore and Pett Pools, is of great interest to the birdwatcher at any time of the year. A wide variety of birds, particularly those favouring a wet-land habitat, can be seen both in the summer and winter. If you wish you can make a short diversion from the route to the Pannel Valley Wetland Reserve where there are hides open to the public.

(1) Cross the stile near the road and the one immediately on the right. Turn left and follow the dyke on the left initially, veer slightly to the right to pass through a gap between two ditches and then continue to a gateway. Go through and head for a gap between two more ditches and continue to another gate. Your general direction should be towards the farm buildings on the hill on the other side of the Level. Head for another gateway, go through and make for the footbridge ahead.

After crossing this bridge walk straight ahead to a wide gated bridge over the Royal Military Canal. Continue ahead making for the right-hand end of a small wood. With the wood on your left cross the stile into a lane.

(2) Turn right and walk along the lane for 275 yards (250 metres), past a white cottage on the right, until you reach a gate on the left, just before the lane passes under the ruins of New Gate, one of the three remaining gates in the town walls. After passing through the field gate look across to the left where Wickham Manor farmhouse can be seen. This is now owned by the National Trust but once belonged to the Penn family, founders of Pennsylvania in the United States of America.

To continue the walk bear right across the field beside a fence to a stile and still bearing right cross a sloping field to another stile on to a fenced sunken trackway. Walk up the track to reach a busy road junction.

(3) Cross the road and turning right walk along the pavement to a T-junction. Turn left - straight on is the centre of Winchelsea. After passing Trojans Platt and St. Thomas's church on the right walk over the cross-roads at the New Inn. At the next cross-roads turn left to reach the A259 road.

Walk No. 4

Site of Windmill, Winchelsea

(4) Cross this road to find a made-up driveway leading to the site of a windmill, blown down in the 1987 hurricane. Go through the gate at the end of the drive and, keeping to the right of the mill, bear right down a sunken track with hawthorn trees on the right. At this point you may wish to pause and admire the splendid view along the Brede Valley. As you continue down the track a gate and stile will come into view. After crossing this stile carry on down the track to a further gate and stile into a field. Walk on the right hand edge below steep slopes and close to the trees.

At the end of the field cross the bridge on the right and bear left over a stile onto a track. Follow this track, which, after passing through a metal gate ends at a road junction. Cross the minor road and follow the pavement on the left of the main road for about 330 yards (300 metres) until reaching the Bridge Inn. Cross the road with care to turn right into a road signposted to Winchelsea Beach. A short distance down this road, after crossing a bridge, turn right through a farm gate signposted "Public Footpath to Pett Level".

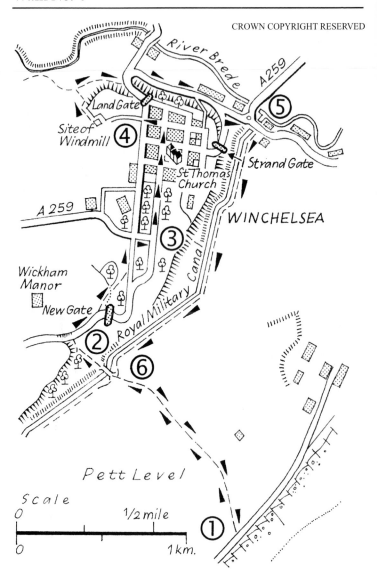

Walk No. 4

(5) The footpath now follows the Royal Military Canal. This canal was built in 1804 to strengthen the defences during the Napoleonic Wars. Walk along beside the canal for one mile (1.6 kilometres) until reaching the wide farm-gate that was crossed in the earlier part of the walk.

(6) Do not cross the bridge but turn left to the small bridge which can be seen across the field. After crossing the small bridge bear slightly right to a gate. Go through and follow the dyke on the right to another gate. From here make for the gap between two drainage ditches and head for another gateway. Continue to a gap between two more ditches and then follow the dyke on the right back to the two stiles leading on to the Pett Level road where the walk started.

Windmill, near Elms Farm, Icklesham

Walk No. 5

Icklesham Circular *6 miles (9.6 kilometres)*

The village of Icklesham is situated on the busy A259 road about seven miles from Hastings. The road runs along a ridge of hills extending from the northern outskirts of Hastings towards Winchelsea.

The walk follows part of the River Brede Valley, and crosses the Pannel Sewer Valley, affording wide rural views. It incorporates parts of the 1066 Foot path and includes seeing a Norman Parish Church, the site of an ancient water driven corn mill, and a preserved windmill.

The village is served by bus, and there is roadside car parking in the vicinity of the starting point.

The walk starts from the Robin Hood Public House **(1)** on the A259 road, at the junction with Watermill Lane. (TQ872162). Cross the road.

With the Robin Hood on the left walk for about 100 yards along the A259 to find Toke cottage on the right, immediately beyond which is a driveway to Lilac Cottage and large gates to Toke Farm. To the left of these gates is a small swing gate with a footpath marker. Through the swing gate proceed along the drive towards Toke Farm house and take the footpath to the left, waymarked on a mushroom-shaped stone. Follow this footpath to join a field, crossing a stile on the way. Once in the field veer away from the left-hand hedge to a marker post in the field and continue in the same direction to a stile at the bottom. Ahead is the Brede Valley.

Cross the stile and, with hedge on the right, walk down the field until another hedge joins it from the right. Turn right. Cross into the lower field and continue with hedge on left down to a stile and finger post at the bottom left-hand corner. Cross the stile and turn left on to the 1066 Footpath. **(2)**

Walk alongside hedge and wire fence on left, at the far end of which is a waymarked stile. After crossing the stile follow the right -hand field boundary to another stile, ignoring a five bar gate on the immediate right. Continue with the hedge and houses on the right , from where a driveway begins. Proceed up the driveway to another stile alongside a cattle grid. On the horizon to the left once stood Telegraph Windmill, a white smock mill demolished about 1922. Once over the stile continue up the driveway, past the house named "Upper Brook" on the right, to a marker post directing the walker to the right, away from some converted oast houses. The diversion to be followed crosses a cattle grid and passes some farm buildings on the left before rejoining the original driveway. After walking a further 50 yards on the driveway it turns sharply to the left. Notice the small brick building on the right at the bend in the driveway - a tar dip for hop and fence posts, still in use. **(3)** Continue walking a further 100 yards along the driveway until reaching a "1066 footpath" signpost just before a pair of cottages.

Take the driveway on the right (keeping on the 1066 route as indicated by the signpost) crossing a cattle grid to pass Snaylham House and The Old Farm House - circa 1630. Just past Snaylham House notice the farm buildings on the left with an outside brick arched stairway and a walled garden. After passing The Old Farm House on the right and a pond beyond it, the walker is confronted by two marker posts in quick succession. **(4)** Turn left at the first post, and walk down the left-hand side of a field for about 90 yards to find an opening on the left into a small copse - in line with the back of the farm buildings.

Turn right and, keeping the hedge on the right, walk down to enter a field. Before proceeding any further look across the valley ahead to a wood and a field. The Right of Way enters the wood at the right hand corner of this field in the valley bottom. For now, keeping the field boundary on the right walk down

to where the hedge starts curving to the right. **(5)** Stop. From here the footpath strikes half left across the field down into the valley and enters a cleft in the wood in the bottom left-hand corner of this field where there is a stream. Cross the stream and follow the well defined footpath up through the wood and out to a field, passing a marker post on the way.

On entering the field the footpath (waymarked) runs parallel to the left-hand side but through the field. At the top of the field join the track 100 yards (91 metres) to the left of a barn and turn right. This track leads to the A259 road **(6)** after passing the barn on the right, a garden centre on the left, and a driveway down to Stocks Farm.

On reaching the road cross over and turn left along the verge for about 100 yards (91 metres) to find a stile and finger-post. Follow the direction indicated towards Pett Church spire. On the way the sea at Rye Bay can be seen to the left, while to the right on the hill is Fairlight Church tower - a prominent landmark in the area. The top of the tower is 618 feet (188 metres) above sea level. Guestling Church tower over 800 years old, can also be seen to the right, nestling in a hollow.

The footpath leads to a waymarked stile at a bend in a hedge. Before

Walk No. 5

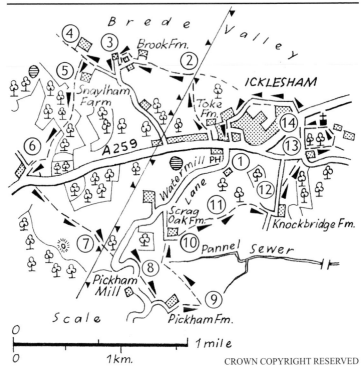

reaching this stile a pylon can be seen ahead a little to the left. After crossing this stile the footpath veers to the left and heads towards the pylon and arrives at a hedge on the left. Walk alongside this hedge for about 130 yards (118 metres) to find a waymark on a fence post on the left.

From here strike across the field and, keeping the pylon (7) to the right, head down to the right-hand corner of a small wood.

The footpath enters the wood and follows the inside edge of the wood down to a stile leading on to Watermill Lane. Notice the Sussex iron fencing on the right and alongside the road ahead.

From here, turn right and walk down the road for approximately 150 yards (136 metres) passing a footpath to the right and another to the left before reaching Pickham Mill (8) on the right. It is known that a mill was working on this

Walk No. 5

site before the Norman Conquest, and was last shown as "corn" on the Ordnance Survey map of 1873. The present house on this site is named Pickham Mill, and, crossing the valley behind it, can be seen the mill bay (dam) behind which was once the mill pond. The stream forms part of the Pannel Sewer (another name for stream). After crossing the road bridge over the stream turn sharp left up the bank (marker on bridge) to cross stiles and enter a field.

Walk up the field as waymarked towards a bungalow with a dormer window. The latter part of the footpath runs alongside a hedge on the left towards and through a farm gate, emerging onto a driveway. Turn left past the bungalow, named Freshwinds, and continue down the drive to Pickham Farm. Keeping the farmhouse and pond on the right, walk straight ahead through an iron farm gate to enter a field. Continue in the same direction towards the far right-hand corner, where there is a rusty farm gate. **(9)** Stop. Staying in this field turn sharp left. Strike across the curved end of the field and head for the left of some trees surrounding a pond to find a stile.

Cross the waymarked stile and veer away from the right-hand hedge to skirt trees on the left. Continue in the same direction to a metal gate at the far left corner beside a stream.

Immediately beyond this gate is a waymarked footbridge on the right. Cross the footbridge and head up the field as indicated, keeping a pond on the left and a spring on the right, to a stile and farm gate into the next field. Continue in the same direction up the field towards a power cable pole with yellow marker between the farm buildings at Scrag Oak Farm.**(10)** Turn right in front of the farm buildings and walk alongside them on the left.

When clear of the buildings veer left to join a farm track and keeping the hedge on the left, proceed to an opening into the field ahead where there is a waymarked stile. Cross the stile and keep alongside the right hand hedge walking past two ponds (ignoring the grassy track separating these ponds). Beyond the second pond a new hedge has been planted, followed by a row of older trees. Where these trees start, **(11)** turn right over a waymarked stile to enter the right-hand corner of a field. Turn left (away from the field division), and walk in the same direction as before, now with hedge and trees on the left. Notice the view. The footpath drops into a valley through a metal gate and crosses a stream. Proceed up the next field keeping a hedge on the right, to the third metal gate which is at the top corner. Once through the gate keep to the left-hand hedge, passing a house and private garden on the left, to arrive at Knockbridge Farm by way of a farm gate.

Turn left through the farmyard and follow the farm drive with houses on the left and farm buildings on the right. Notice the alterations that have taken place over the years to the old barn on the right. Walk up the drive for 150 yards (136 metres) to an iron gate on the right, just beyond a pond and a tree **(12).** Once through the gate veer away from the drive (which is to the left) and head for a stile in front of three fir trees seen between two houses. Cross the stile and walk diagonally across the field through the gap in a barrier fence to find a farm gate and stile in the corner. Whilst crossing the field notice the tower of the Norman church at Icklesham to the left, whilst to the right can be seen

Hog Hill Windmill, saved from dereliction by a local farmer about fifty years ago.

On joining the road at a "T" junction **(13)** notice the road sign, each finger corresponding in length to that of its wording - typically East Sussex. Cross the road junction to a power pole, and turn right over a stile onto and along a driveway alongside the house numbered TWO. Follow the driveway past some garages to another stile into an orchard (ignoring the stile on the right) to arrive at the other side where, 30 yards (27 metres) to the left of a farm gate in the corner, will be found a stile leading to a driveway.

Turn left along this driveway - part of the 1066 footpath - keeping

Walk No. 5

alongside the orchard and on to a grassy track. Continue along the track, but in order to visit the ancient church turn right at the next fork in the path.

The 13th century church is large, denoting its importance in former times. There are impressive Norman arches and columns, and a single roof covers the nave and both aisles. The nave and the chancel are not in line with one another - a not uncommon feature. Attractively worked hassocks add a decorative feature to the traditional pews. Amongst the graves in the churchyard is an ancient yew tree.

On leaving the church retrace the few steps to rejoin the 1066 footpath and turn right along this path to join Workhouse Lane. Just before doing so look to the left over a stile **(14)** at the view of the orchard, oast houses and Hog Hill Windmill - very much a Sussex scene.

Once on Workhouse Lane follow the footpath sign to the right noticing the old school and house en route, to join the A259 road.

Cross over the road into Parsonage Lane, past some attractive dwellings, a short distance behind which was once an early iron works - a bloomery. The Queens Head Public House (built in 1632 as two dwelling houses) is set back on a bend of the lane. Continue along the lane to the right of which can be seen the Brede Valley, Rye, and the North Downs. Where this lane becomes a footpath, follow it along the hill top, with gardens on the left, ignoring the finger post which directs the 1066 footpath over a stile into a field on the right. Instead keep on the hilltop path - still alongside back gardens - then at the next fork in the path bear right and shortly enter a housing estate.

Proceed along the road ahead and take the first turning on the left to arrive at a "T" junction. Directly ahead is a signposted footpath which leads to the A259 road at a house appropriately called "The Ramblers". Turn right for a short road walk to the "Robin Hood" public house.

27

Walk No. 6

Rye and the Brede and Tillingham Valleys
7½ miles (12 kilometres)

This walk, starting and finishing at the ancient Cinque port of Rye, is to the west of the town and takes in the valleys of the two rivers, the Tillingham and the Brede which come together at Rye and flow into Rye Bay. For the most part the walking is easy and there is the possibility of a lunch break at Peasmarsh if desired. The route followed is anti-clockwise.

There is a train service from Hastings to Rye and also a regular bus service. It is suggested the car-user should park at Gibbet Marsh car park, which is on the western side of the town just off the road to Udimore and Broad Oak. The walk starts from the car park.

Turn right out of the car park and walk eastwards for about 150 yards

Rye Harbour and Windmill

Walk No. 6

(135 m) along the road towards Rye town centre. Immediately after crossing the bridge over the River Tillingham climb the stile on your left and follow the bank of the river for about 50 yards (45 m). Where the brick wall on your right bears sharply right, cross the meadow diagonally right to the raised, paved footpath, which continues along the bank of the river. Leave the paved footpath at the next stile and turn left along the raised embankment.

This part of the route follows the High Weald Landscape trail and the signs are helpful in following the route.

(1) Just before the farmhouse turn left and cross the meadow to the stile in the hedge ahead. Climb the stile and follow the river on your left to the end of the field where there is a gate on your left. Go through and turn right to follow the dyke on your right. The dyke turns a corner to the right. Leave the dyke at a line of poplar trees on the right and continue across the meadow to a field gate ahead. Your general direction should be towards the red barn, which can be seen on the hill ahead.

Once through the gateway bear left and keep close to the raised embankment on your left, which is probably the remains of a pre-existing hedge. Follow the bank to the gateway, which is close to the

river. Go through and follow the hedge on your right to the end of the field. Go over the footbridge and stile into the next field.

(2) Continue up the hill keeping to the fence on your right and making for the red barn. On reaching the barn continue along the clearly defined track, which passes through Clayton Farm until it reaches the road.

Turn left along this quiet country road, which passes Peasmarsh Church of St Peter and St Paul on your right. There has been a church on this site for nearly 1000 years and the earliest parts of the present building date back to about 1070, just after the Norman Conquest.

A look round the church is recommended and should you wish to have a refreshment break go through the right hand gate in the churchyard as you look down on Peasmarsh in the valley. The path goes straight down to the village where there is a public house, which serves food.

(3) Continue along the road from the church, passing Peasmarsh Place on your right. At the road junction take the turning to the left. Follow this for about 270 yards (250 m) and then turn left down the drive leading to Pelsham Place, ignoring the road, which swings round to the right. At a fork in the

Walk No. 6

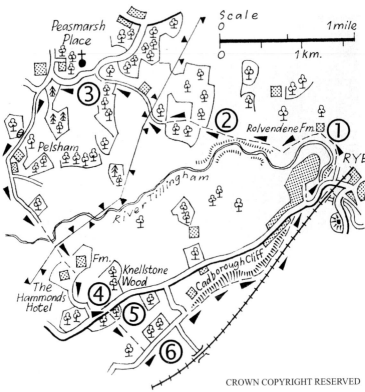

drive, bear right through high iron gates in a brick wall. Pass a lake on the right, then Pelsham House to the left and go on through Pelsham Farm. Follow the farm track, which can get muddy in rainy weather, passing Hookers Wood on your left. The track ends at a farm gate as you enter the Tillingham valley. Go through and cross the valley, going over the river at Tillingham Bridge. Head towards the buildings at the top of the hill, keeping the fence on your right-hand side. As you reach The Hammonds the path goes through a galvanised gate and swings round to the left skirting the gardens.

Follow the hedge until the path meets a farm-track when you should turn right. Continue along

30

Peasmarsh Parish Church

this track as it winds its way up the hill to the main road.

(4) Turn left along this busy road. It is suggested that you walk along the wide grass verge on the right-hand side, facing the traffic. After about 270 yards (250 m) you reach a house on the right. Take the path on the right immediately after the house and follow it through the wood and to a stile into a field.

(5) From here there is a wide panoramic view over the Brede valley. Winchelsea is straight ahead and farther to the left the squat outline of Camber Castle.

Aiming for Winchelsea Town, cross the corner of the first field to a stile and then across a narrow field to another stile. Continue in the same

general direction, which takes you between two electricity pylons, and head downhill across the field. After about 290 yards (270 m) you will reach a stile. Cross this and the next narrow field out to the road by another stile.

(6) Turn left along the road for the final part of the walk. Follow the road ignoring the turning off to the right, which leads to Winchelsea station. About 270 yards (250 m) beyond the turning, the road you are following, called Dumb Woman's Lane, turns sharply to the left. Leave the road at this point and go forward along the cycle track, which runs along the foot of Cadborough Cliff. Follow the track back to the main road and to the car park where the walk started.

Walk No. 7

Flackley Ash (Peasmarsh) Circular
5¾ miles (9.25 kilometres)

Originally Flaeccan Leah - Flaecca's Woodland Clearing. By 1724 when the name Flackley Ash appeared it is thought a large ash tree nearby acted as a local landmark.

To approach Flackley Ash take the A268 road from Peasmarsh to Beckley. Shortly after passing the Cock Inn on the left you will see the Flackley Ash Hotel sign on the right and a road (Mackerel Hill) leading to Wittersham. There is a three-cornered grass island, with a large willow tree and verges on which to park cars nearby.(1)

To commence the walk, cross the A268 and bearing slightly right enter Mill Lane and just past the white house on the right, turn right into a field and follow the path that goes diagonally across it, then go past some polythene tunnels to a gap in the trees - walk round the left hand edge of the next field to a stile and foot-path sign. Continue straight ahead through a plantation of young trees towards a footpath sign. Climb the stile into the wood and follow a well-defined path straight ahead, keeping the outer fence of the wood on the left, towards another stile and footpath sign. Bearing right, follow a rather overgrown path (alongside a garden) down to a stile **(2)** and then turn right along a gravel lane,

passing Woodlands Farm on the left. Further on, pass between a large red barn and four silos and follow the lane round to the right and then turn left into Houseropers Wood, by the footpath sign, **(3)** and follow the well-trodden path which meanders through the wood. It is reported that some wild boar live in the woods, behind the double wire fences.

At the crossing of two footpaths continue straight ahead through a swing-gate into the Sussex Wild-life Trust Nature Reserve (Flatropers Wood) and continue to follow the path ahead. Crossing a bridge over a small stream, ignore the path on the right and continue straight ahead over several board-walks and under some power lines and follow rhe path which meanders through the wood until a swing-gate (alongside a 5 Bar gate) leads into Bixley Lane **(4)** Bear slightly left and follow the unmade lane for approx. a quarter mile (400 metres) until you see a footpath sign on the right. Climb the stile into Bixley Wood **(5)** and continue straight ahead (it is rather overgrown through the bracken at times). Note a way-mark sign when you reach a clearing then continue north alongside a wire fence on the right-hand side. Note

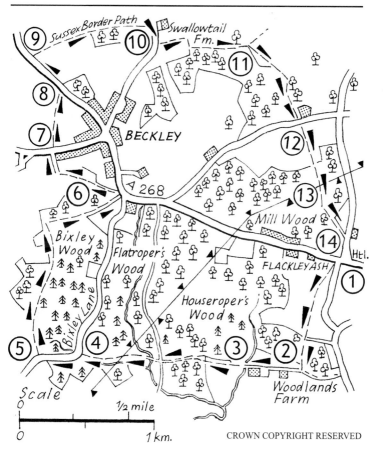

Scale

0   ½ mile

0   1 km.

another way-mark sign on the left and continue straight, ignoring the path that branches right, and follow other way-mark signs (this path can be overgrown also), until you reach a finger post. Turn right here and follow the path for some distance before going through a gap in the fence (way-marked) and continuing straight ahead. When you see a gate ahead into a lane, ignore this, but turn sharp left and follow the path up the incline and then eventually down to a stile. **(6)** Climb over this, then turn sharp right along a path with a wire fence on the left-hand side. Continue by following the path round the edge of the field, (ignore the first stile on the right leading back into the wood), to an over-grown stile and turn right down a path through trees to the main road.

(7) Bearing right, cross the road then left over a stile, alongside a picket fence, and walk through the meadow, passing a way- mark sign on a telegraph pole towards a gap between a hedge and clump of trees (another way-mark sign here) then continue ahead, keeping to the left-hand side of the field, to a stile (8) leading, into a very busy road (see the sign on a post) Turn left along the road *with extreme caution*, past the Woodlands Guest House and just past the bend in the road turn right onto the (9) Sussex Border path which climbs to a stile on the right. Crossing the stile, turn left up a field to another stile and continue up towards a wood passing a large tree on the left. Go over the stile and through the copse and an open field towards another stile. Once over this turn right along a wide grass path, noting the fine un-interrupted view over to the left and the seats and hedge of roses on the right-hand side.

At the end go through a five bar gate (10) and turn right down the lane past Swallowtail Farm. Just past the two cottages on the left turn onto the Sussex Border path and keeping to the left-hand side of the field, follow the path down to a gate and then turn right and follow the path round the edge of the field and over a stile into a wood.. Follow the path through the wood, across a stretch of field to another stile with a yellow post, then passing a pond on the left (11), continue down through some trees to another yellow foot-path sign and then straight ahead alongside a fence towards a gate. Go through this and then continuue diagonally up the incline past the way-mark posts amongst the trees (this is part of the High Weald Landscape trail) to a metal gate in the right hand corner. Continue through a small swing-gate and then another large gate onto the road.

(12) Turn right, then opposite the"Old Shepherd" turn left up some steps and over a stile into a field. Cross to a finger-post and then down towards a stile and into a plantation under some power lines and continue ahead to a further stile and into Mill Wood. (13) Follow the path and when a fork in the path is reached, take the left-hand path (see sign-post) and continue up the gradual incline to a finger-post and out onto the road. Turn right past "Mill Wood" and back to the start of the walk. (14)

Walk No. 8

Westfield Circular *5 miles (8 kilometres)*

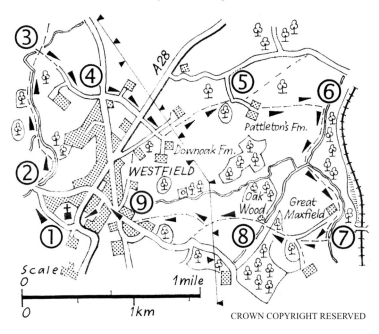

CROWN COPYRIGHT RESERVED

Westfield lies just north of Hastings on the A28 road. If you are coming from outside Hastings the A28 turns left off the A21 just before you enter beneath the bridge on the town outskirts. Westfield lies a mile or so down this road and your walk starts at the very beginning of Westfield village.

(1) Park in the lay-by behind the War Memorial at St John's Church in Vicarage Lane. Walk down the lane to Wheel Lane and then turn left briefly up the lane leaving Wheel Cottage on your right and enter the large parking area beside Wheel farm, a small complex of light industries.

(2) Keep the stream on your right and you will shortly pass a bridge on your right. Keep on bearing slightly left to reach a steel gate with a waymarked stile (ESCC and 1066 Country Walk) Go over the stile into the field and head towards an electricity pole on the right. Continue with the stream on your right to another stile and gate,

35

carry on in the same direction to yet another steel gate and stile with waymark and after a short distance another gate and stile leading you into a large field with a sign post. Walk on beside the stream until it turns at a right angle across your path and you can cross the wooden bridge. Continue in a straight line until you come to a stile and sign post on your right.

(3) Turn right and go over the stile and up the field at 90 degrees to your previous course, eastwards. After 40 yards (37 metres) cross a wooden stile and proceed up the slight slope to the top left hand corner, keep the hedge to your left. You will pass some tall oaks on your left before entering a lane and then emerging into a further lane. Bear left and go up the lane past Little Westbrook farm and on into Westbrook Lane, turn left and be careful crossing the road (Cottage Lane) to a triangle of grass with a postbox and sign "Westfield".

(4) Leave the road behind you and proceed up the lane opposite until you cross the main road, A28; cross with care. Carry on up the lane (sign for Downoak and Southings Farm). Where the lane forks enter the corner of the hedge between the entrance for Downoak Farm and the lane on the left. Cross the small grassed area and exit over the waymarked stile (1066 path). Walk down to the gate in the bottom

right hand corner of the field, at this point you are walking past the end of the back gardens of a group of houses and will shortly emerge into a field. Keeping the hedge on your left go down the hill to a gate and stile, go diagonally right up the next field to a stile in the hedge. Over the stile continue towards the right hand corner, cross another stile and into the lane where there is a triangle of grass where you may pause to get your bearings. Take note of the commemoration engraved on the crossbar of this stile to the Hastings Rambling Club Golden Jubilee.

(5) Go right down the lane, pass a house on your left, go through a steel gate with another house on the left with a blue farm cart in the garden, then pass a garage on your right. Turn sharp left and go over a stile (you are now at Pattleton's Farm), aim to pass between the two trees. Go diagonally across the paddock to a stile in the corner (waymarked), go over the stile and straight ahead over the crest to a small wooded area with a signpost. Carry on down to a sign-post on the riverbank - indicating the 1066 Country Walk and the 1066 Hastings Walk, Icklesham is 3½ miles straight ahead - and turn right walking with the stream on your left (Doleham Ditch).

(6) Walk along the field with the river on your left until you come

Walk No. 8

Maxfield Manor

to a waymarked bridge over the stream. Go left over the bridge and up the path bearing left to a stile and gate. Go over the stile and into a long field with a cottage/barn in the top left corner. Walk out of the field through the gate near the barn into the lane to meet a sign post indicating three paths.

Facing you is Great Maxfield. Most of this building dates from the late 16th. century, but the great chimney stack is probably late 14th. century. For many years the house stood empty and gradually decaying but has now been restored to the delightful building we see today. Maxfield Manor was the early home of Gregory Martin, born about 1514, a Roman Catholic theologian who escaped from England during the religious persecutions in 1570 to Douai in

Flanders where he translated the Bible into English from the Latin Vulgate, the translation being known as the Douay version.

Go right up the lane, past Great Maxfield Barn Farm passing houses on your right and along a metalled road with a lake on your left until you reach a minor cross roads.

(7) Turn right and go due west alongside the large field with the field boundary on your right and the ditch on your left. After about 136 yards (125 metres) you cross a stile on your right into the field and continue to the top right hand corner of the field, (aim for the electricity pole). Walk alongside and then turn left into the copse keeping to the right hand side inside the trees and after a short distance you emerge into a field - carry on

Walk No. 8

down the field, crossing a track, to the bottom keeping the hedge to your right and enter the wood by another electricity pole. Walk along under the wires to reach a stile leading into a narrow field, cross this and exit over the stile into a very large field.

(8) Your route will generally head west, (follow the electricity poles) until you pass under the pylons and cross the brow of the hill still heading in a westerly direction, (the hedges that for generations marked the line of the footpath have been demolished). Aim for the electricity pole and clearly marked path in the next field, you will find a stile beside a dead tree in the hedge row that lies across your path. Cross the stile and carry on over the field under the electricity wires to the hedge opposite with an iron gate. Follow the signposted path through a small field and lane to emerge into the minor road almost opposite the Plough Inn, a good stop for a meal or a refreshing drink.

(9) From this point turn right and walk up the road to Westfield taking the left hand fork. Continue until you reach a turning on your left marked "Heathland" and walk to the end where you will see an entrance on the right that leads you out past the tennis court to the road side almost opposite the War Memorial and the entrance to Vicarage Lane and the start of your walk.

Golden Jubilee Stile, near Pattletons Farm

38

Walk No. 9

Sedlescombe Circular *5 miles (8 kilometres)*

The walk explores the Brede Valley and the undulating countryside to the North East of the village, including woodlands and a glimpse of Powdermill Reservoir.

The village of Sedlescombe is situated on the B2244 road, just off the A21, some six miles to the north of Hastings. The main street is on the course of a Roman road which linked Hastings with Rochester. An old pump under a gable-roofed shelter forms an attractive feature on the green which is surrounded by picturesque houses, some dating from the 16th and 17th centuries.

Over the years local industries have included sheep and cattle farming, iron workings since Roman times and the manufacture of gunpowder from 1761 to 1874. In '1959 the Pestalozzi Children's Village Trust was established on the outskirts of Sedlescombe. Here children from many countries are educated in the British way of life, whilst maintaining their own traditions.

At the top of the Village Green is the Brickwall Hotel and the Queens Head Public House. Running Between the two is Brede Lane, along which is a Car Park **(1)** with toilets . There is also a bus service (No 254) linking the village with Hastings.

The walk starts at the foot of the village green, opposite Gregory Walk. Take the footpath on the left indicated by a stone marker, which runs between some dwellings.

After a short distance the footpath makes an "S" bend, beyond which it crosses a footbridge and leads to a kissing gate into a field. To the far right can be seen the Pestalozzi Children's Village. Follow the well-defined footpath straight ahead to the far left corner of the field, to find a gate and stile into another field. Once in this next field walk alongside the left-hand hedge, at the end of which is an iron kissing gate. Passing through the gate the footpath is fenced on both sides with a children's play area on the left. At the end of this section of the footpath do not turn left into the housing estate, but cross the stile and continue in the field keeping hedge and gardens on the left.

Continue alongside this left-hand hedge and cross a stile, driveway and another stile into the next field. Still keeping to the left hand boundary, walk ahead to find a footbridge into the next field at the far left corner.

Shortly it should be possible to see Brede Pumping Station Engine Houses in the valley ahead - the home of a triple expansion steam

Walk No. 9

engine built in 1904, which along with other engines and machinery, is being lovingly restored to working order by enthusiasts. The pumping station is open to the public at certain times.

Keeping to the left boundary of the field as before, follow the footpath to a second footbridge. A little further on there is a stile **(2)**. Lower Jacobs Farm **(3)** can be seen ahead. After crossing the stile keep to the left-hand edge of the field, as signposted, to the corner; the footpath borders a wood on the left all way to Brede Lane. Turn right - again as signposted - along the second side of the field to a stile and footbridge still keeping alongside the wood on the left. Turn sharp left following the edge of this next field again alongside the wood to cross another stile. Ahead is yet another stile on to Brede Lane.

Turn right past the farm but look out for the different coloured brick work of the house on the left, with its extension and bricked up doorways. **(3)** Follow the lane down to and across the valley for about a quarter mile (500 metres) to find a footbridge leading into the field **(4)** on the left at a right-hand bend in the road before a wood. Cross this footbridge and walk along the side of the field, keeping a stream on the right. Note the furnace slag underfoot, more noticeable at the farther end of the field. Soon the footpath crosses another footbridge. Continue, still keeping to the right hand side of this large field (once three individual fields). Towards the end of the field the right hand boundary and stream bear to the right. At this point there is a marker on a fence post. From here the footpath strikes diagonally across the last part of the field to the far left-hand corner where there are double wooden gates out to Powdermill Lane. **(5)**

Turn left for 70 yards (64 metres). On the way notice the high grass-covered bank in the field on the right. This forms the dam to Powdermill Reservoir (formerly known as Great Sanders) which is managed by Southern Water, and along with Darwell Reservoir at Mountfield, supplies the Hastings area. Near the dam there was once (circa 1578 until mid 18th Century) an iron works furnace, hence the slag in the field. The furnace was later converted to a powdermill, the remains of which were destroyed when the reservoir was built between 1929 and 1933 by Hastings Corporation Water Works. A few steps after passing a driveway to a house and the reservoir, cross a stile on the right. Follow the signposted footpath half left through the wood. The footpath is well-defined and crosses some fallen trees, then passes under power cables and runs alongside a private garden on the left with another house on the right. Before reaching the end of the garden **(6)** the footpath turns half right - once signposted - into a wood of fir trees. After 12 yards (11 metres), the path crosses a disused track and continues straight ahead to a

Walk No. 9

Sedlescombe Parish Church

waymarked stile. Cross the stile and bear slightly right onto a well-worn track leading down to and across a footbridge. Many of the fallen trees are the result of the 1987 hurricane. From here the footpath meanders through the wood (Wards Wood) for about three quarters of a mile (1.2 kilometres), crossing two more footbridges. After the first of these footbridges the reservoir may be glimpsed through the trees to the right. Beyond the next footbridge the path climbs steeply and by way of a stile into a densely-wooded area - which can get very muddy - emerging over a stile on to a fire-break (a wide clearing in the wood). Here bear left as waymarked down the firebreak between tall pine trees

to cross a stream at the bottom. Turn left (7) immediately over two footbridges along the waymarked footpath, which follows the stream. Notice the rust-coloured water, a sign of iron ore in the ground. Continue along the path to another fire break. Turn left again and follow the footpath to yet another fire break. Again turn left at finger post and pass through a farm gate with stile to enter a large field (once several individual fields).

Walk straight ahead keeping a cluster of nine hop poles on the right (8) and aim for the right-hand end of a small wood seen at the top. From this wood a hedge and row of trees stretch down into the field

Walk No. 9

towards you. Keep to the left of the hedge to find a stile and gate at the top leading out to Hurst Lane **(9)**, on a sharp bend. There are footpath marker stones on each side of the road.

Cross the road and take the footpath opposite, keeping to its left-hand hedge or fence to arrive at an unmade road with dwellings. Turn right along the road to where it makes a sharp left-hand bend. **(10)** At this point leave the road and walk straight ahead into a copse, to find a small iron gate on the left leading into a field bordering the unmade road. Here the view, with Sedlescombe Church on the right, is worthy of a pause. **(11)**

Keeping to the left-hand hedge proceed down to a swing gate leading into a second field. Still keeping to the left walk down to the next hedge where there is another gate. Ignoring the stile on the left pass through this gate into a third field and again keep to the left hedge. At the bottom pass through yet another gate to arrive in a fourth field.

Continue walking in the same direction with the hedge now on the right to arrive at a wooden swing-gate leading onto a rough road. Walk down this partly-concreted road passing properties on the left to find a stone marker at a footpath to the left - immediately before Balcombe Green Cottage.

Turn left down this footpath to emerge into a housing-estate. Turn right down the road - Orchard Way - then left into the next road to return to Brede Lane opposite the car-park.

Walk No. 10A

Cackle Street, Brede, Circular by way of Arnold Bridge
5 miles (8 kilometres)

Beckley Furnace Farm

This walk which starts and ends in Cackle Street, Brede (8 miles [13 kilometres] north of Hastings on the main A 28 road) goes through some undulating countryside with fine views.

At the top of Brede Hill go through the village, noting the interesting old church of St George on the left and the Red Lion Public House on the right, continue along the road and at the next junction, here is Cackle Street. Some distance along the road there is a sign indicating the Village Hall opposite and just past this there is a lay-by under some tall trees. There is a sparse

bus service between Hastings and Northiam which stops nearby.

To commence the walk go through a **(1)** metal gate and walk diagonally left across the field towards a finger-post near a pond. Turn sharp right here and continue towards another metal gate at the end of the garden of a bungalow. Go through this onto a path which runs behind the houses in the main road - continue along this path until you reach a ladder-stile, go over this and continue walking slightly diagonally right towards a gap in the hedge and a small stile and gate. From here continue along by

Walk No. 10A

a wood and pond and bear sharp right to another ladder-stile onto the A28 road.

Turn left on to the pavement and after 22 yards (20 metres) cross the road towards a new red-brick house (with a "private" sign), go through a small metal gate, past four garages to another metal gate ahead. Continuing through the gate follow the fairly well-defined path, keeping the fence and hedge on your right. Cross another stile into the next field and follow the path downhill, still keeping the fence on your right, to the next metal gate. Go through this and follow the grass track which ascends the hill towards **(2)** Moorsholm Farm and bends round to the right through the farm, between the farm buildings towards a five-bar gate with a foot-path sign. Go through the gate and down a grass track for approximately 35 yards (32 metres) to a finger post. Turn left here and cross the field towards a gap in the hedge with another finger post, about 30 yards (27 metres) to the right of the field gate, then head towards another metal gate. Go through this and cross another field towards a stile alongside a gate and head down the field, roughly towards the electricity pylon, with a view of a white house over to your left, to another stile. Cross this and take the small sunken path (beware of rabbit holes) as far as a tarmac

drive. Turn right here and continue uphill as far as the main road, noting a converted oast house and a barn on the left-hand side.

Turn left and cross Goatham Lane, then immediately opposite go down a rough track as far as a stile between two gates. Climb the stile and walk down the centre of a long field to another stile in the right-hand corner. At the time of writing, this stile needs repairing. Continue ahead down the next field, keeping the trees on your right and cross the bridge at the bottom, over the stream, then turn sharp right and walk along the valley to a stile in the corner of the meadow, between two wire fences (another one requiring attention). Continue along the left-hand side of the next field and climb the stile on to the main road at Arnold Bridge **(3)**.

Almost opposite take the long wide track, past a white weather-board house on the bank to your left and further on, a view of a lovely old house across the fields to your right. When the track branches, take the right-hand path past a white weather-board bungalow and cross over a small foot-bridge. Continue ahead along the next field, keeping the stream on your left until you reach a bridge on the left. Cross this and turn right along the worn path, alongside the stream, to another stile and footbridge. Cross over and continue along the stream for

Walk No. 10A

approx. 66 yards (60 metres) before you climb a stile into Wagmary Wood. Follow the winding path through the wood (which can be overgrown during the summer months), passing a finger-post on the right, confirming the route of the path. At the end of the wood, cross the ditch and climb a stile, then follow the path between the

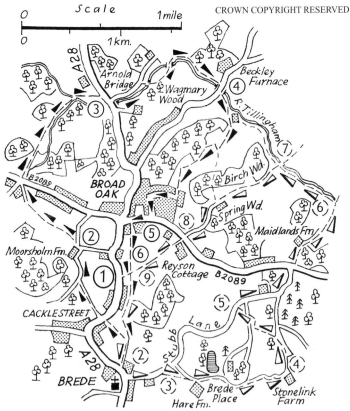

Map for Walks 10A and 10B

Direction signs and numbers for Walk 10B are shown thus:

stream and the paddocks, keeping the fence on your left, towards **(4)** Beckley Furnace, noting the iron deposits in the stream. From pre-Roman times to the age of the Stuarts this was part of the great iron-smelting area of East Sussex and the Kentish border, hence the origin of the name Beckley Furnace.

To continue your walk, cross the stile into the lane then opposite follow the tarmac drive to Furnace Farm and the Log Cabin. Proceed past the barns and the Log Cabin then climb the hill to a stile, alongside a gate. In former times there were hop gardens here but these have disappeared during the past 15 years. Cross the stile and continue up the field, keeping the hedge on your right, then cross another stile to a finger-post, turn sharp right and walk as far as another finger-post before turning immediately left across the field towards a wood. Pause here and admire the view down the lovely Tillingham Valley towards Rye. Turn left again and walk along the edge of the wood and around the corner to a metal gate. Bearing slightly right, with the wood still on your right, continue climbing towards a small metal gate, then turn left up towards some bungalows, keeping to the left -hand side of the field until you reach another metal gate. Go through this and follow the path

between some gardens and past a small electricity sub-station, into a housing estate.

Turn right and follow the road round to the T-junction at the end of Fieldway. Turn left and continue along Reedwood road as far as the main Rye road **(5)** Cross the road then turn right past the Methodist Church and Brede Primary School and continue until you see a phone-box on the right-hand pavement. Immediately opposite is the footpath down to the left past the ruins of a tumble-down cottage, however if the path is still blocked by the local authority, owing to the danger from the cottage it is suggested you should walk to the cross-roads and turn left to take the paved path beside the road, which will take you back to your starting point.

If the footpath is clear then proceed down past an electricity sub-station to a stile, go over this and continue straight ahead, past Sunbeam Farm Cottage on the left and some farm buildings on the right and follow the track down to another stile, continue down the next field to a metal swing-gate leading into a copse. Follow the well-defined path through the copse until another metal gate is reached. Go through this and head for the finger-post and diagonally right across the field back to **(6)** the starting point of the walk.

Northiam

River
A 28
A 268

River Rother

7

Beckley

Peasmarsh

RYE

Broadoak
River Tillingham

6

10

Udimore

Brede

River
Brede

Camber Castle

5

Winchelsea

Icklesham

4

A 28

A 259

Royal Military Canal

Westfield

8

Guestling

Pett

3

2

Fairlight

1

HASTINGS

Scale

| 0 | 1 | 2 | 3 | 4 Miles |

| 0 | 1 | 2 | 3 | 4 | 5 | 6 Kms. |

Walk No. 10B

Cackle Street, Brede, Circular by way of Brede Place
& Maidlands Farm *5 miles (8 kilometres)*

This walk starts from the same lay-by at Cackle Street on the A28 road, as in the previous walk.

To commence, go through a metal gate **(1)** and walk diagonally left across the field towards a finger-post, near a pond, turn sharp right here and continue towards another metal gate, at the end of a garden of a bungalow. Go through this gate onto a footpath which runs behind the houses in the main road - continue along this path until you reach a ladder-stile, go over this and continue walking slightly diagonally right towards a gap in the hedge and a small stile and gate. Go through and bear slightly left across the field, skirting a copse, to a stile and note that on the horizon one can see the tower of Fairlight Church (one of the highest points in Sussex and visible from several places on this walk). Proceed straight ahead across another field, keeping to the fence on the left, to a swing gate, go through and then down a footpath, past a long fence and by a chalet bungalow to the main road.**(2)**

Turn left and then left again down Stubb Lane. Continue along the lane for approx. half a mile (800 metres). Thirty yards (28 metres) past the 30 mile speed limit sign and just past an oblong brick

building on the left, turn into the wood on the right by a stone footpath sign **(3).**

Follow the well defined path through the wood and across a tarmac driveway towards a swing gate - go through this and note the superb view across country on the right and Fairlight Church again visible on the horizon. Continue ahead down the next field, keeping a wood on the left and on down hill to a stile, alongside a gate. Go over this and proceed downhill to another gate through to Hare Farm and cottages on the right. Turn left past some farm buildings (note a footpath sign on the barn) and go through another gate by a tall tree and continue downhill along the left-hand fence to a bridge across a stream, then begin to climb up a field past Brede Place, rebuilt after a fire in 1972 had destroyed the 14th - 15th Century Manor House.

Pause here to admire another superb view on your right before continuing ahead through two metal 5-bar gates onto a tarmac driveway. Go ahead to another gate then turn immediately left and walk alongside the fence and then turn right downhill (with a hedge on your left) to a stile near a stream (it is always rather wet here). Cross this and continue by climbing a steep grassy hill, with a hedge on the left, to a stile and then on up to a swing-gate onto the driveway to Stonelink House and Cottage. **(4)**

Turn left along the driveway, passing Stonelink Farm on the right and a timber-clad cottage on the left and about 130 yards (118 metres) from the barn bear left across a grass verge down to a stile in the hedge with a sign post alongside. A few paces over the other side of the stile go down to a small plank bridge and up into a field. Continue up the field beside the left-hand hedge for approx. 60 yards (56 metres) then where the hedge turns sharp left go diagonally right across to the hedge opposite. Keeping beside the hedge on your right, follow round past the garden of a house to a stile on the right over a wire fence. Cross the stile and walk ahead to another stile and follow the grass track round to a further stile. Once over this, pass a large oak tree on your right then continue straight ahead between two oak trees and then past some young oak trees and bear diagonally left down towards a driveway. Turn right up the drive, past a bungalow on the right and by the last tree on the

Route Consultation   Photo: Richard Dymond

Walk No. 10B

left (opposite the hedge) walk diagonally across the corner of the field reaching a stile behind a large oak tree, leading onto the lane opposite the entrance to Broadland Harbour.

(5) Turn right and proceed along the lane for half a mile (800 metres) until the main Udimore road is reached by the 50 mile-limit road sign. Cross the road towards an old cottage and a sign to Maidlands Farm. Turn right down past the cottage on a rough driveway and left of Maidlands Oast and where the driveway branches, take the right-hand track and continue down-hill, past a cottage on the left, as far as a metal gate. Climb the fence to the right of the gate and continue diagonally left down-hill, aiming just to the left of some taller trees in the hedge ahead to a stile with a footpath marker on it. Climb this stile and then a second one and head diagonally right across to the river. **(6)**

On reaching this, turn left and walk along the river bank, noting the man-made lake on the left-hand side and continue until you see, slightly to the left, a stile and wooden bridge - cross here and continue along the track near the river bank until you come level with a wooden bridge crossing the river from the right-hand bank. Turn immediately left here and follow the track **(7)** across to a stile, climb this and begin to ascend the hill alongside Birch Wood on the right.

Continue until you reach a stile, climb over and head diagonally right towards another stile. Ignore the gateway opposite and turn left towards another gateway under a tree, with a stile alongside and continue up the field, keeping the fence on your right until you reach another stile in the corner of the field. Climb this and turn immediately left up the field, with Spring Wood on the left. Go through the gap at the top of the field, follow the track round to the left then go through a 5-bar gate and turn right along a driveway until you reach the main Udimore road again.

Bearing slightly right, cross the road to **(8)** Reyson Cottage, go through the metal gate and down the field alongside a fence. At the end of the fence branch diagonally right down towards a gap in the trees, cross the stream then ascend the slope towards another gate and follow the well defined track across the field. Go through the gap in the hedge then turn right along the side of the next field, past a pond on your right towards a finger-post and on reaching this, follow the track back to the metal gate **(9)** and the starting point of the walk.

Walk No. 11

Bodiam, Sandhurst Cross and the Rother Valley
5 miles (8 kilometres)

Bodiam Castle

This pleasant walk starts from the picturesque Bodiam Castle, crossing into Kent and returning by way of Sandhurst Cross into the Rother Valley and up river to the Castle again.

This moated castle was possibly built as a defence against raids by the French in the 14th century but was never put to the test and was later plundered by the Parliamentary Forces during the Civil War. In 1926 the castle was bequeathed to the nation by Lord Curzon of Kedleston and now belongs to the National Trust.

It is certainly worth a visit in conjunction with your walk.

(1) The walk starts at the Castle car-park. Leave by a gate into the grounds and go across the small field to the left of the castle as you face it, and make for the ticket office and museum just behind it.

Go past the ticket office towards the left-hand corner of the field ahead of you and climb over the stile on your left. Continue uphill by a well-defined path with hedges on either side and eventually alongside a fenced field on your left. If you

Walk No. 11

look back at this point you will have a fine view of the castle in the valley together with rising fields opposite and the spire of Ewhurst Church on the far horizon.

At the top of the hill go past the oast-houses on the left and turn left over a stile and then right past trees and a hedge, across a concrete driveway and over a stile into a small field.

Continue downhill for a short way and bear left alongside fencing and trees on your right until you come to a stile and gate by a large oak tree. This route is part of the Sussex Border Path. On climbing over this stile you will notice ahead in the distance a steep hill with Sandhurst Church perched at the top.

However, you continue diagonally left across the field, downhill

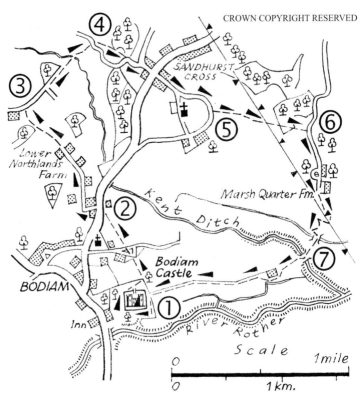

towards two white houses, and at the bottom, the road. Cross this and immediately turn left onto a narrow roadway. After a short distance this road bends sharply to the right.

(2) Continue along this road rounding several bends as far as Lower Northlands Farm. Follow the track through the farm by way of the wicket-gate ahead. The track now becomes rougher. You pass a bungalow on the left, climb a stile where the track drops down slightly and continue along the edge of the wood and a field fence until you reach a junction of paths which is close to Northlands Farm.

(3) Turn right at the junction and follow the trackway downhill. Avoiding a bend to the right, continue in a straight direction past a wood. The wood ends at the bottom of the hill where you cross a small field and over a stream by a footbridge. Keeping the stream to your right walk a short distance and cross a tributary stream over an earth bridge and a stile into an open field. Turn left following the same stream and hedge to the end of the field where there is another stile leading onto a narrow roadway.

(4) Turn left and immediately right through a gate. Turn right again and pass through another gate into a narrow strip of woodland and over a small stream. Climb up a steep bank by steps into an open field.

Head across the field to the top of the hill, aiming for the right tip of a wood which is clearly seen ahead. From here you have a good view of the surrounding countryside. The Kent Ditch Valley and a row of dwelling houses at Bodiam can clearly be seen together with the route you have just walked. Continue in the same direction across this field downhill and make for the left-hand side of the white house and buildings ahead. Leave this field by a stile and join the roadway again. Go uphill along this road and continue when it merges with another road. This shortly meets the Bodiam road at Sandhurst Cross. You go straight across to the road opposite. Follow this for about a quarter of a mile (400 metres) when you will come to a fork. The right-hand road leads to the Parish Church of St Nicholas which was seen earlier on your walk and which you may wish to visit. Your route, however, is along the left-hand fork. Walk along this road, which curves round to the right, until you are fully in line with the eastern side of the church.

(5) Turn left by a concrete waymarker and over a stile, heading eastwards across the field towards another stile at the opposite end of the field. Climb this and continue into the next field, heading in the same direction, roughly towards an electricity pylon.

Walk No. 11

Crossing over a stile in a hedge walk straight ahead to a wood. Go over a stile to the left of the pylon and follow the path in the wood which shortly bends to the right and arrives diagonally at a stile on the left leading into an open field.

Head downhill across the field diagonally to the right in the direction of another wood and through an opening into a farm lane.

(6) Turn right along the lane for about a quarter of a mile (400 metres), passing farm buildings and houses and finally go into the open field at the end of the lane. Cross the field bearing left downhill to a pylon and hedgerow. Beyond this go into another field. Go right and follow the edge of the field. This will take you past two left-hand corners. On the final stretch, turn right just past a large bush and over a footbridge across a tributary of the Kent Ditch. Continue along the bank of another wide ditch towards a high bank ahead. This is the Kent Ditch which is the county boundary into Sussex.

(7) Cross the Ditch by a substantial footbridge, passing a pumping-station on your left and continue in the same direction along a broad track. This continues for about a mile parallel to the River Rother. Soon you will see the familiar profile of Bodiam Castle ahead. This track will take you back to the castle grounds and your starting-point.

Welcome committee! Marsh Quarter Farm, Bodiam area

56

Walk No. 12

Battle Town Circular *4 miles (6.5 kilometres)*

This is a short ramble which covers some of the historical buildings in the town, and takes the walker around the perimeter of Battle.

The town was originally a village of shops and servicing industries which grew around the Abbey. This was built by William the Conqueror in atonement for his soldiers who were killed in the year 1066, at the Battle of Hastings. From medieval times the town has more or less maintained its form to the present day.

(1) The walk starts at the Abbey Gates, a fine facade of period structures ranging from the west wing in the 14th. century to the East Courthouse, built in the 16th. century. In 1338 the whole structure was fortified and crenellated as a defence against possible incursions by marauding French soldiers. The licence to do this was granted by King Edward III. The court house had a variety of uses but until recently was left as a shell. Now under English Heritage the whole building has been refurbished with a roof and accommodation made for an assembly hall and visitor reception and shop on the ground-floor. The Tourist Information Centre is also housed in the same premises.

Standing with the Abbey gates behind, you view the whole so-called Abbey Green. The Pilgrim's Rest, immediately on your left, is a fine example of a Wealden Hall House, a common structure in this area in medieval times, and in Battle in particular. Reputed to have been in existence since the twelfth century, to accommodate pilgrims visiting the Abbey, it was rebuilt in its present form in the early 1400's. The building was restored in the 1930's and is now a restaurant.

To the right of the Pilgrim's Rest is a row of early buildings containing shops and small cafes, also a large coaching archway which was originally an inn but closed in 1850 with the coming of the railways. Just past the post office is the 1066 inn, which also had a coaching entrance, but is now rebuilt as interior space for customers. This inn was originally called The Star, and two centuries ago shared with the George Hotel the stopover for the Royal Mail coaches between Hastings and London.

Looking to your immediate right you can see Buckley's Museum and a series of Wealden Hall houses with stucco facades. These comprise the Abbey Hotel and more shops. Almost opposite the Post Office and next to Lloyds Bank is the Battle Memorial Hall, or Langton House, which was built in the 16th. century with

Walk No. 12

general additions and refaced in the 18th. century. The main assembly hall was built in the last century and used for various activities. From here is the High Street, the main centre for shops , inns and restaurants. Most of these buildings were constructed in medieval times and later refaced in the 18th. century which was a popular style of architecture then.

Continuing on the left side of the street is Steamer Trading, a hardware shop which was originally Thorp's shoes shop, a long established trade here which supplied boots to the troops in the Napoleonic Wars. The actual building was probably constructed in the 15th. century together with early additions. Further along on the same side is another coaching archway. Through this is the Old Brewery Yard. The original brewing factory is still there but now accommodates offices.

On the right of the High Street, opposite, is a refreshment area with a characteristic multi-pane glass fronting. It was built in the time of Charles II and later refurbished in the following century. Continuing from here is a newsagents and estate-agents. The original buildings suffered a direct hit from bombing in the Second World War, and were rebuilt afterwards. These show an attempt to keep within the original styles although the reconstruction was in the 20th. century.

Further along by the butcher's shop is Abbey Court, a small, newly constructed pedestrian area of shops and dwellings, with a steel banner curved overhead by the entrance and reading "Newberry Preserves". This was the site of the jam-making factory established in the 1880's. Continuing on the left of the High Street is a multi-paned shop window which has been preserved since its construction in the 1800's. This shop is at present owned by Battle Luggage. Next is an entrance to a privately owned car park, belonging to Clements Shop

next door. These premises were the original Till's ironmongers, and reputed to have been the oldest ironmonger in the country. Further along the street, situated by Moss, the chemists, notice a very narrow bow-fronted building, referred to as a "squeeze" house.

One of Battle's main centres is the George Hotel. Originally an 18th. century coaching inn, it has now become an Italian Restaurant on the ground floor with separate hotel facilities in the remainder of the building. On the same side of the street is another inn, now adopting its original name "The Bull". Constructed at the end of the 17th. century from stone salvaged from the ruins of the Battle Abbey kitchens it now looks distinct from the other buildings which are made with locally sourced bricks and tiles. Opposite on the right is a converted late 19th. century chapel, long neglected and now a restaurant. At the junction is Mount

Street which was the original road to London until a more direct route was built in the 1830's. A distinctive row of Wealden Hall houses can be seen on the right of this street, including the Old Kings Head public house. Ahead in the distance is Lewinscroft, a large 16th. century timber structure and now converted into a series of dwellings and sometimes nick-named "The Rabbit Warren"! Near to the High Street and left of Mount Street is a towered building with three round-arched windows, originally the town's blacksmiths but now converted to shops.

Beyond this junction on the left of the High Street is the Guild Hall, fronted in the18th. century. Part of this building has a medieval undercroft, and possibly secret passages, now blocked, to the old Abbey.

The next building is Martin's Oak with a small plaque indicating

Battle Abbey Green

Walk No. 12

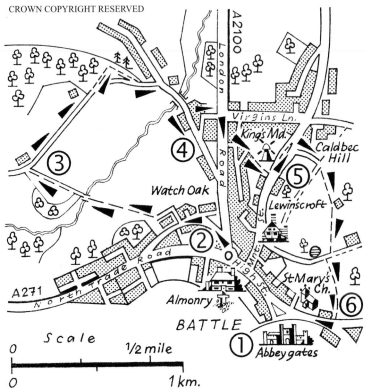

the year 1748. Finally there is the Almonry, an excellent example of early Hall house structure, with gardens open to the public. This now accommodates the Council Offices, restaurant and a separate building for the Battle museum.

Opposite on the right are characteristic early tiled buildings and a series of new apartments, addressed as Rue de Bayeux.

These were built on the site of the Old Wellington Inn, the original sign of which can be seen in the courtyard.

The High Street ends at the roundabout and on the left is the Market Place complex. This new area comprises shops, dwellings, a supermarket, bandstand and a library, all built on the site of the old cattle-market.

Walk No. 12

At the roundabout take the main London Road to your right and at the first turning on your left go up a slip road **(2)** and follow this into a new housing development. This area is known as the Watch Oak. Continue to the end of this road where it suddenly narrows into a lane. Turn immediately right, down a track way which soon bends to the left. Arriving at a large gate and stile, cross this into a long field and aiming for the farm buildings in the distance, walk directly downhill towards a wood and a footbridge over a stream. Crossing this bridge follow the footpath into another field and go uphill parallel to the hedge on your right.

(3) Cross the stile by the gate at the end of the field and turn right into a roadway. Follow the roadway, noticing the windmill high up over the fields and trees in the distance. After about 550 yards (500 metres) turn left along a track in a wood. Walk a short distance into this wood and follow the trackway where it bends sharp right and eventually arrives at the roadway again. Turn left on to the roadway and this will take you to the main Netherfield road. Turn right and follow the road over a bridge and uphill. Near the top of the hill take a sharp left turn into a small residential road called Wattles Wish. **(4)** This curves to the right and through a pedestrian way onto the main London road.

Take care when crossing as there is plenty of traffic.

On the opposite side is Virgins Lane and a residential estate to the right . Turn right onto a grassy bank until you see a stile and a concrete way sign to the left in the hedgerow. On the other side is a tarmac footway. Follow this to the right and continue as it bends to the left and comes to a roadway. Cross the road and continue in the same direction, up a series of steps, across another roadway and into a twitten and an opening into a field. This area is called Kingsmead and above Harold would have gathered his troops prior to the great Battle. Continue uphill with the thick hedgerow to your right, then turn right through a gap into another field. At the top of this field is an old concrete triangulation column and a seat.

Take the opportunity to rest and admire the expansive view over to Netherfield. In the distance you can just see Netherfield Parish Church and also the route of your walk from the Watch Oak. Just beside you over a hedge is the Old Mill, an easily seen landmark from almost all areas around Battle. The mill is privately owned and not open to the public. Pass through a metal gateway beside the mill onto a gravel footpath and driveway and go down towards the main Caldbec Hill road. **(5)** Turn left uphill until

61

you come to a large grassy area. Note a large timber-structured hall-house on your left. Now called Wellington House, it comprises two dwellings but was originally the Kings Head Inn until the London Road was opened in 1830

Towards the end of the grassy area cross to the opposite side of the road and follow a narrow driveway to your right leading to Caldbec Cottage. The driveway has a high brick wall on the right and dwelling-houses on the left. Continue downhill towards a kissing-gate and into a field. Keep in the same direction following a high hedgerow on your right. In the far corner, by a wooden signpost, cross over a ditch into a large field.

Here is one of the best views of Battle. Looking from the left you can see the Great Wood, then nearby is the Marley Lane junction with Upper/Lower Lake by the Chequers Inn. This will be the next destination in your walk. Looking to the right is the Parish Church and the profiles of Battle Abbey and the rooftops of Battle High Street silhouetted against the sky. Also far right are the allotments and a shorter route back to town.

However, you should aim across this downwards-sloping field just to the right of the nearby cottages. Pass through a wide gap in the hedge and follow the driveway

until it makes a sharp curve to the left. This is where you bear right across the field going downhill to the bottom right-hand corner, roughly in the direction of the Parish Church ahead. At the bottom is a farm-track. Turn right along the track and then almost immediately left, by a large clump of bushes and a stream , into a small field. Head for a gap in the line of trees skirting a stream. Cross over this by a footbridge and veer left uphill towards the left side of an isolated tree. At the top continue down to the bridge with handrails and then into the next field. This is called Lake Field and belongs to the National Trust. The pathway from here takes you up a steep slope and through a gate onto the main road. This is the junction between Marley Lane and Upper Lake, part of the 1066 Country Walk. Take a look back at the route which you have just followed . You can admire the expansive view over the fields to Caldbec Hill and the Old Mill, partly hidden by trees.

(6) On the road opposite is the Chequers Inn, one of Battle's oldest buildings, and to the right is a row of medieval terrace houses, originally almshouses built as part of the Abbey. After the Reformation these became places of ill-repute. Later they developed into proper dwellings, some shops and a residential education centre, known

Walk No. 12

as Pyke House. These buildings were timber-structured throughout, then in the 18th. century the frontage was refaced as seen to day.

Turn right by the metal signpost and bus shelter and proceed up the hill in the direction of the town centre. As you pass a row of cottages on your right you will see one is indicated as the Abbot's House. This is where the last Abbot of the Abbey came to live after the Dissolution in 1538. Continuing further, on the same side, is the Battle Parish Church of St Mary the Virgin. It is a medium-sized church with its expected beauty, enhanced inside by a series of restored wall paintings underneath the clerestory.

Across the road is the high perimeter Abbey wall, built in the 14th. century for the defence of the Abbey against incursions by the French. Following this wall on the left, you finally arrive at the starting-point of your walk.

For more information on this historical town, please refer to the Battle Town Trail, which is featured in the official guide and obtainable from the Tourist Information Centre.

Battle, from Caldbec Hill

Walk No. 13

Battle Circular via Petley Wood and the River Line Valley
5½ miles (9 kilometres)

Walking towards Caldbec Hill, Battle

The walk starts and finishes at the Mount Street car park east of Battle High Street. This car park is reached by turning at the parking signs from the High Street into Mount Street.

(1) Keeping to the left of the car park turn into a footpath by a bungalow called "Little Twitten". Continue until a grass track is reached and cross the track with Battle Town Council Gardens on the right. Continue with the allotments on the right and go through the swing gate into a field. Walk up the hill, keeping the hedge on the left. Turn left before the cross hedge, going over a wooden plank bridge and turn right at the sign post. Keeping the hedge on the right follow the path to the stile into the Nursery and go forward to cross the next stile into Uckham Lane.

(2) Turn right along Uckham Lane, past Fuller's Farm on the left and cross the railway bridge over the main London-Battle line, and on reaching Coarsebarn Farm bear left leaving the buildings to the right. Go over the stile in the hedge on the left and walk diagonally across the field to the power cable pole and then down to a ditch at the bottom of the field and over a stile. Bear slightly right walking beneath the power cables, keeping one pole to the left and the rest to the right. Rutherford Business Park can be seen ahead in the distance. Continue across the field to a wide gap in the hedge and follow the track keeping a hedge on the left until meeting a cross hedge. Go through the opening on the left, walk diagonally across the field and down the slope until you reach a stile on the right. There is an equestrian centre here. Continue past the stables into Marley Lane.

(3) Turn left along the road, past the road signs for a short distance and turn left into a well-defined track with Dene House on the corner on the right. Follow the track past Little Squirrels House on the right and continue as it narrows into Petley Wood. Continue up the hill till meeting the deer fence and turn right for about a quarter mile (450 metres) through the woods. On reaching a track pass in front of the barn and continue down the sunken footpath to the left. On reaching a sign post continue round to the left on footpath 46. Go downhill and turn right at the footpath sign

leading to the plank foot-bridge across the River Line.

(4) Turn sharp left keeping the river on the left. Cross two fields to a cart track through woodland and then with a vineyard on the right. Cross left over a wide bridge; turning right keep the hedge to the right until reaching Whatlington Village Hall Car Park and the Whatlington Road.

(5) Turn right , cross the road to a stile and cross the field diagonally right to a stile and footbridge crossing a stream. Follow the path keeping the river to the right through four fields, crossing five stiles until reaching a small wood. Continue until there is a footbridge crossing the stream to the right.

(6) Turn sharp left opposite this footbridge, walking diagonally up hill to the top of the hedge on the left parallel to power lines and follow the track and footpath to the railway bridge. Continue straight on to Woods Place.

(7) Turn sharp left along the track for a short distance and then right towards two low brick farm buildings. Walk to the left of a building along a narrow path, under a lean-to with an asbestos roof. Cross the stile and keep straight down the hill, through a large gap in the hedge to the bottom of the field . Turn left over the bridge

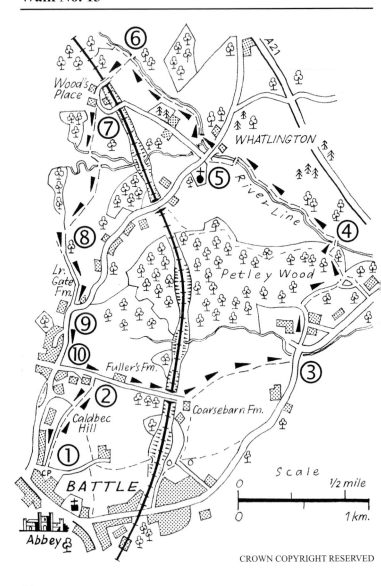

CROWN COPYRIGHT RESERVED

Walk No. 13

and cross the next field to another bridge over the river which is diagonally to the right. Go straight up the hill under the power lines to a stile at the top of the rise and continue in same direction to a stile in the hedge. Continue in this direction across the field to a stile to the left of Lower Gate Farm.

(8) After crossing the stile, turn sharp left between the hedge and the barn and go over a stile onto a track. Follow this track till Gate Farm and the Whatlington road is reached.

(9) Turn right towards Battle and keep on the right hand side of the road until reaching Virgins Lane.

(10) Turn left across Battle road into Uckham Lane and continue until the footpath sign and over the stile into Uckham Nursery. This rejoins the route followed on the outward journey. Continue straight on along this footpath until the plank footbridge on the left. Cross the footbridge and turn right continuing along the footpath, past the allotments on the left until a cross track is reached. Continue back to Mount Street Car Park and the start of the walk. Battle can now be visited for refreshments.

Whatlington area

67

Walk No. 14

Robertsbridge Circular with a taste of the Sussex Weald
6 miles (9.6 kilometres)

This walk, of about 6 miles (9.6 kilometres), is to the north and west of Robertsbridge and offers pleasant walking through typical Wealden landscape with attractive views over valleys and gentle, wooded hills.

Robertsbridge is about 10 miles (16 kilometres) from Hastings and can easily be reached by train and car. There is a public car-park on the left if you turn from the main street to go west to the railway station. The walk starts from the car-park.

(1) Turn left along the road from the car-park and walk to the station - about 440 yards (400 metres). Go over the level-crossing and just beyond the first house after the crossing take the path to the right. (If arriving by rail turn right out of the station and take the path on the right just beyond the first house). Follow the path which skirts a wooden fence on the left (ignore the path to the left) until you reach a stile. Climb over and walk through the field following the fence and railway embankment on your right. Cross a small stream by a plank bridge with stiles at each end and continue, passing the tunnel under the railway on your right, to the stile and plank bridge just beyond. Cross the bridge and turn right up the narrow field to the opening at the end.

(2) Turn right through the opening and climb the hill keeping initially about 20 yards (18 metres) from the right-hand hedge. Go over the stile in the fence crossing the field and go towards the hedge on your right where you will find a stile into the next field under a large oak tree. Go over the stile and follow the hedge on your left. Proceed to the corner of the field and climb the stile. Advancing slightly to the left follow the path between two hedges downhill to a plank bridge and stile under a large oak tree.

(3) Cross into the next field and head diagonally left uphill across the field . At the top of the hill you will be able to see Squibs Farm ahead. At this point veer to the left and go towards the hedge on the western side of the field. There is a stile and footbridge in the hedge 30 yards (27 metres) to the left of a gap and 100 yards (92 metres) to the left of the brick bridge in the corner of the field. Go into the next field and walk up the hill towards Hackwoods Farm. Go through the gap in the hedge and follow the hedge on your left to the corner. Ignoring the path on your left go through the gap in this hedge into

Walk No. 14

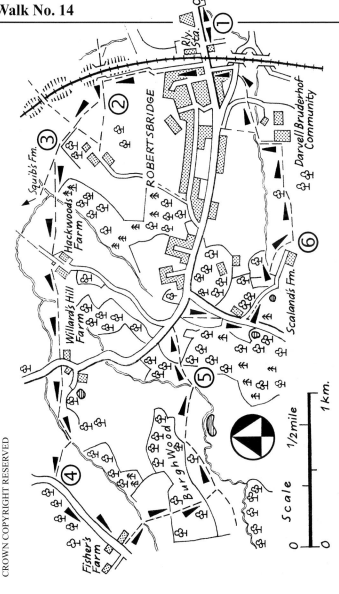

① R/y. Sta. C.P.

② ROBERTSBRIDGE

③ Squib's Fm.

Hackwoods Farm

Willard's Hill Farm

④ Fisher's Farm

Burgh Wood

⑤

⑥ Scaland's Fm.

Darvell Bruderhof Community

Scale

0   ½ mile   1 km.

69

the next field . Follow the edge of the garden on your left to the top of the brow then walk diagonally across the field to two stiles (currently dilapidated but there is a gap adjacent) in the hedge ahead. Your general direction should be towards the oast-houses just visible ahead. Cross into the next field and go in the same direction to the corner of the field.

Just to the right of the corner you will find a bridge at the foot of a bank and partially hidden by trees. Cross the bridge and follow the hedge on your right almost to Willards Hill Farm .Go over the stile on your right , turn left and follow the line of buildings on your left. Cross the ditch and go to the corner of the field where there is a well-made path which leads round the building and on to the road.

Cross the road and go through the gate opposite into the field. Follow the left-hand hedge until you reach two small fenced enclosures when you should go through the gate and downhill diagonally to the bottom hedge. Follow this hedge almost to the corner of the field. You will find a stile and bridge on the right hand side close to an electricity-pole. Go over the bridge into the next field and follow the hedge on your right uphill until you reach a gateway. At this point cross the field diagonally left heading for the coppice in the top left corner.

Climb the stile, follow the path through the coppice and past the pond out to the road.

(4) Turn left along the road for about 600 yards (550 metres) until you reach Fishers Farm on the right. Take the track on the left just beyond, and just after the farm buildings, and follow it to the field ahead. Once in the field walk uphill to the top left-hand corner. Climb the stile and enter Burgh Wood. Continue in roughly the same direction through the wood. The path is sometimes indistinct but it is not difficult to find the stile on the far side.

Climb this into a field which runs down into a pleasant and secluded wooded valley. Follow the hedge on your right to the gateway at the bottom and go through into the next field. Turn immediately left and follow the hedge along which runs a raised green track. Go to the end of the field, through a natural gap and over an earth bridge and then continue uphill in the next field keeping close to the line of trees and ditch on your left. At the top of the hill there is a fence and stile. Cross this into the next field and go forward keeping to the hedge and ditch on the right-hand side. Follow this to the bottom corner of the field.

(5) Descend by path under the trees and through undergrowth to the stream where you will find a bridge. Cross this and continuing in the same general direction cross the meadow in front of you. Pass through a field gate, over a plank bridge and go towards the wood ahead. Walk a few yards alongside the edge of the wood and climb the stile into it. Turn immediately right and follow the well-marked path up the hill through the wood until you emerge into a field through a wicket-gate.

Continuing forward in the same direction go to the gateway in the corner and then into the next field. Keep to the left-hand side of the field and go to the gateway which leads out to the road.

Turn right along the road for about 130 yards (120 metres) and then turn right just past the house and garden over a stile into a field. Walk through the field keeping near the hedge and wood on your right-hand side. In the far corner climb the stile on to the road. Turn right along the road for about 215 yards (200 metres) and then turn left down the farm track to Scalands Farm.

Continue down the track for about 325 yards (300 metres). Before Scalands Farm, which is ahead of you, climb the stile on your left into the field and head for the kissing-gate in the fence ahead. This is just to the left of the hedge skirting the farm-house and garden. Go through

the gate across the grass track and through the field-gate. Follow the path which skirts the hedge and garden on your right to the kissing-gate into the next field.

(6) Turn left in this field and follow the fence on your left to the gateway into the next field. Continue forward with the hedge on your left to the kissing-gate which takes you into a wooded area. You are now in the grounds of the Darvell Bruderhof Community. Follow the hedge on your left until you reach a track which you should follow round the left-hand side of the Community buildings.

The Darvell Bruderhof Community was established in 1971. The members live a simple communal life earning their livelihood by making children's toys and producing food from their own farm. They are one of several linked communities of Anabaptist Christians in America, Europe and Australia.

Go down the hill and past the stables and farm buildings. Follow the farm track for about 55 yards (50 metres) beyond the buildings and then turn left through the gateway and over the bridge. After a few yards turn right through a field-gate into a field. Follow the right-hand edge of the field which runs along a wood. Go through the gate at the end and across the metalled drive.

Walk No. 14

Go through the gap in the hedge opposite into the recreation field. Continuing in the same direction walk down across the field to the gate in the left-hand corner near the children's play area. Turn right along road and almost immediately left to take the footpath into the housing-estate. The path joins a road (Mill Rise) which you should follow through the estate and out to Station Road at the end. Turn right along road, over level crossing and back to your starting-point.

Walk No. 15

Crowhurst Circular *5½ miles (9 kilometres)*

Crowhurst is a small village lying between the western outskirts of Hastings and the historic town of Battle. It is easily reached by car and the main Hastings - London railway-line runs through the outskirts of the village. Parking for car - users is available at the railway station but this is likely to be limited on week-days.

The walk is to the west and south of the village and can be accomplished fairly easily in half a day. It is particularly enjoyable in Spring when the bluebells in Fore Wood are a delight.

Start at the station and walk down the road to the church. A stop to admire the church and churchyard is recommended. There has been a church on the site since the 8 th century but the actual fabric has been restored several times, the last being between 1960 and 1970. The yew tree on the southern side of the church is reported to be at least a thousand years old.

Crowhurst, 13th century manor house and parish church

If you go into the churchyard and past the church entrance you can follow the path round to the gate on the northern side. You will then emerge on to the road you should follow.

(1) Turn left along the road and follow it until it turns sharply to the right. Ahead is a fieldgate which you should go through and follow the hedge on your right-hand side. This section of the walk follows the 1066 Bexhill walk and the signs can be followed to the end of Fore Wood. Where the hedge turns sharply to the right go straight ahead and make for the corner of the field. Follow the hedge on your right and near the corner go down a broad track between a hedge and a coppice. Where the track goes into a field bear slightly to the right and follow the path to the wood ahead.

(2) This is Fore Wood and is owned by the RSPB. It is managed to encourage a wide variety of woodland birds, butterflies and flowers.

Follow the undulating track as it winds its way through the attractive coppice woodland, ignoring paths to the left and right. You finally leave the wood by crossing a substantial wooden bridge with metal rails and emerge into a field. Cross the field to the woodland on the other side and then turn right along a path through a gateway to a metalled lane. There is a house on the other side of the lane at the junction.

(3) Turn left up the lane and eventually go past Forewood Cottages on the left. From this point the lane is unmetalled and as it emerges into a field it becomes a sunken farm track. Continue down the track and then along the lane into which it merges. This passes a pond on the right and continues uphill passing a farm on the right and Catsfield Place on the left. At the top of the lane is the Crowhurst to Catsfield road.

(4) Cross the road by the signpost and walk across the field in a south-westerly direction making for two holly trees which are at the right-hand end of a more or less continuous line of trees which lead to a house at the left-hand end. Go through gap by the holly trees into the next field. Follow the hedge, then a wood on the left and over a stile into an adjoining field. Continue in the same direction with the wood to your left until it stops at a corner. Cross the open field, bearing slightly to your right, to the corner of another wood. On reaching this continue along its edge to the corner of the field. Dipping to the left into the wood, climb over the stile and continue along a winding path through this wood. As it nears the road you skirt the garden of a house on your right

Walk No. 15

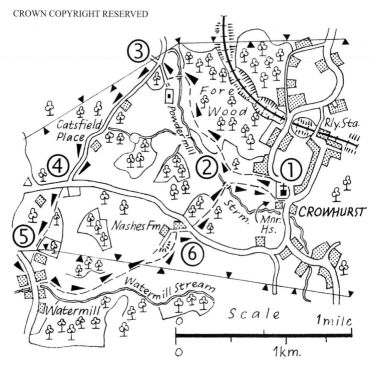

and there are farm buildings on the left on the other side of a small stream.

(5) Climb the stile at the end to emerge into Watermill Lane. Turn left along the lane for about 200 yards (180 metres). Immediately past Rose Cottage turn left over a low wall and through a wire gate. Follow the path between gardens and climb stile into field. Follow fence on right to another stile. Go over and follow fence on left for about 140 metres to another stile. Climb this and follow fence on right to bridge and gate. Go through and foward to hedge at the end where there is a plank bridge and stile. Go into the next field and cross it diagonally to the hedge on the left aiming for the large electric pylon on the skyline.

Go over a ditch by an earth bridge and about 20 yards (18 metres) beyond it in the hedge on the left you will see a squeeze. Go through

74

Walk No. 15

into the next field and follow the left-hand hedge. Just after passing under an electric power line turn right across the field to a stile in the opposite hedge below a small coppice. Climb stile and follow hedge and fence on left for about a 100 yards (90 metres) to a stile and plank bridge. Cross into next field and head north-eastwards keeping the farm buildings of Nashes Farm well to your left. As you reach the brow of the hill head for the corner of the field where there is a big house on the skyline.

(6) Climb the stile and steps up to the farm track. Turn right and walk along to the road. Cross the road to the stile opposite and go into the field. This commands a spectacular landscape view in the direction of your walk. Initially keep to the

right-hand hedge in this field and after about 60 yards (55 metres) cross the field diagonally to the bottom of a group of trees on the left. From here you can clearly see below the meadow and a gateway and bridge, where you will follow through and continue your walk. Go over the bridge and bear right diagonally uphill making for the end of a coppice on the skyline. From here continue along the winding hedge to a gateway into the next field . From here you can easily see the church and the ruins of the 13th. century manor house ahead. Cross the field making for the gateway just to the left of the old Manor house. Go through, past the ruins and out to the road. The road up to the station and your starting point is now opposite.

Fore Wood, Crowhurst

Walk No. 16

Sidley Circular by way of Crowhurst
5½ miles (9 kilometres)

This is a gentle walk through the valley of the Combe Haven that lies between St Leonards on Sea and Bexhill. Although so close to built-up areas, it remains remarkably quiet and unspoilt.

For the railway enthusiast, it is possible to trace the route of the Bexhill West Branch Line, which ran from Bexhill through Sidley to Crowhurst and was closed by Beeching in 1964.

It is convenient to start the walk at Sidley car park, which is behind the shops in Ninfield Road. There is a [P] signpost to the car park from the road and also a sign indicating that it is a recycling centre.

(1) On leaving the car park turn right and pass through Sidley's small parade of shops. A bit further on, reach a road-bridge crossing a disused railway line.

(2) The petrol filling station on the other side of the bridge occupies the site of the former Sidley railway station booking office from which steps once lead down to the platforms below. Railway enthusiasts might like to read a booklet, "The Bexhill West Branch Line", written and published by Peter A. Harding (ISBN 0 9523458 6 2).

On the opposite side of the road to the petrol filling station, turn left at the road juction and after about 30 yards (27 metres) turn left again down a footpath signed "Crowhurst 2½ miles".

Further on, this takes you between the disused railway cutting to the left and a housing estate on the right, coming to a field at the end. Climb the stile and cross the field towards a metal barn of Glover's Farm.

Leave the field by another stile, turn right and go down a well used path between barbed wire on the right and a hedge on the left, passing along the southerly edge of Glover's Farm.

(3) The route now continues in an easterly direction. Pass behind a gate and cross over a broad grassy track to the stile opposite. After the stile, go straight on with a fence to the right, and then bear off to the left through the field between some domestic electricity supply pylons to a stile in the hedge on the opposite side.

Over the stile the path leads into a new plantation of beech and oak, with a hedge to the right. The path through here can get a bit overgrown in the summer. At the end of the plantation, go straight on through a cultivated field to a six-bar gate leading onto a lane.

The lane is sign-posted "1066 Bexhill Walk". Keep straight on eastwards past some farm buildings to reach Little Worsham Farm on the right

(4) Take the left fork in the track, sign-posted "Crowhurst 1¾ miles". This takes you in a northerly direction. Go straight on at the next three turnings. Then a stile beside a seven-bar metal gate leads to a crossing of the disused railway line, with another stile and seven-bar gate on the other side. After this, veer right across the corner of a field and pick up a hedge on the right, descending into the Combe Haven Valley. There's a stile at the bottom.

(5) The path now crosses the flat valley with its reed beds. A couple of footbridges carry you over streams.

It is a good time to stop and contemplate. Can you hear any sound? Perhaps there's a dog barking in the distance. Maybe you disturbed some frogs that hopped, frightened, back into their pond. Not a sound of traffic. Turning to the right and facing eastwards down the valley, it is possible to see on each side the two railway embankments that were once joined together by a 17 arch viaduct that spanned the valley at this point. Imagine steam engines puffing and belching smoke as they crossed.

(6) Moving on in a northerly direction, the route bears over to the right and goes alongside a small stream at the base of an embankment. It passes two farms up on the hill to the right, first Adam's farm and then Croucher's Farm.

(7) Passing under the National Grid power lines, the route approaches Crowhurst alongside a playing field.

This is the halfway point of the ramble. Here are seats for a picnic, swings for the children and a pub, "The Plough", for the grown-ups.

You may like to explore the village of Crowhurst. It has a Church and the remains of a 13th Century manor house. The Old Rectory houses the Crowhurst Christian Healing Centre. (See www.crowhursthealing.co.uk)

(8) Start the return journey by taking the steep path to the left of "The Plough" pub. At the top, turn right into the road, past Hye House. Then, at the junction with the major road, turn left. Take the opportunity to cross the road, watching out for traffic, and look down the bank on the opposite side at the picturesque view of the church below.

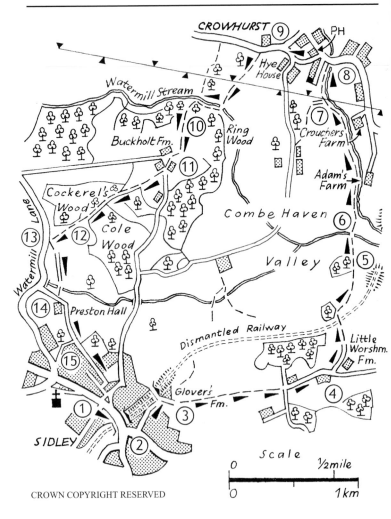

(9) Now it is necessary to travel along the road for about 275 yards (250 metres), watching out for traffic, to a bridleway signpost on the left beside a domestic electric pylon. Sometimes this signpost gets overgrown with ivy, so look out for it carefully. The bridleway gets you off the road and runs downhill with a hedge on the right to a pond.

Through a seven-bar metal gate there is a hedge to the left of the path, continuing downhill under National Grid pylons and through a six-bar gate. Go forwards to a stream with cascading water, Watermill Stream, and pass through two more seven-bar gates. After the stream, the path leads off to the right. Pass through another seven-bar gate to enter Ring Wood.

(10) The track through Ring Wood goes uphill and bears round to the left. Don't take any side turnings. Leaving the woods, go straight on uphill through a field to a stile beside a gate. Have a look backwards at the fine view. The footpath now leads clockwise around to the back of Buckholt Farm.

(11) Climb the stile beside a gate into the farmyard. You might like to have a look at the very old farmhouse on the right.

Do not be tempted to go forwards down a very long straight track, which is in fact a private road, but turn left at the farmhouse. Then, shortly after passing a pond on the right, go through a gate in the fence on the right leading into a small field. Bear left in the field,

pass a second pond to the left and make towards a stile that is visible about 44 yards (40 metres) away. After the stile the path runs in a southwesterly direction, with a hedge to the left.

After another stile, skirt round to the right of the wood and go down a small incline to a rickety footbridge over a ditch. Go straight ahead up the other side to a gate with a stile beside it. In summer bracken and nettles may obscure the stile and sometimes the gate is left wide open.

The path continues straight on, with a wood to the left, into a triangular field. Towards the end of this field, with Cole Wood to the left, the footpath veers off to the left into a twitten. Then, leaving Cole Wood behind, the path runs on in the same direction with Cockerel's Wood to the right.

At this stage in the ramble, one might think of all the wild flowers that have been seen. There might be bulrushes in the ponds, bluebells in the woods in the spring, irises in June and blackberries in the autumn.

(12) From Cockerel's Wood, the footpath veers to the left into the field, making for a stile in a hedge leading to Watermill Lane. The stile is just below a white cottage with a cockerel on the roof.

Walk No. 16

(13) Do not cross the stile into Watermill Lane but turn about and look for another stile in the fence opposite, exiting to the south of the field. The path now runs in a narrow twitten between two hedges, ending at a stile and a footbridge over a ditch. Cross a field, going up a small hill, to reach a lane beside a farm and a very large heap of manure. Turn left into the lane towards Preston Hall.

(14) The track continues in the same direction towards Sidley, passing through a recreation ground and a small wood before reaching a housing estate.

(15) Keep straight ahead through the houses to get back to Sidley's shopping precinct and return to the car park.

Walk No. 17

Brownbread Street, Ashburnham Circular
6¼ miles (10.16 kilometres)

Brownbread Street is a small hamlet about 6 miles (10 kilometres) west of Battle. To reach it take the A271 road from Battle and continue along it past Ashburnham Park. At the end of the Park take the first turning to the right and after half a mile (approx. 1 kilometre) turn left along a narrow lane and at the next junction turn right to reach the hamlet

This walk commences by the Ash Tree Inn, a useful place for refreshments at the end of the walk.

(1) Walk a short distance north along the road, noting some unique terraced cottages on your left called "Longhouses", with a decorative brick structure and a row of dormer windows for four dwellings. There is a stile on your left, way marked,

Long houses, Brownbread Street

easily noted as there is a large typical Sussex farmhouse called "Suttons" opposite on your right. Pass through this stile down a thick-hedged footpath to a following stile and on to a river bank flanked by trees and hedges on your right.

Cross over this through a gap in the hedges into an open field. Continue alongside the stream and trees on your left over a dip in the field and bear left towards another stile, which is in the fence to the right. Cross over this and walk directly across the field bearing slightly to your left. At the opposite end of the field you will arrive at a right angle corner of the edge of a wood. Continue in the same direction alongside the wood and a fence to your right. Almost immediately you come to the end of this field and need to climb over the fence on the right and pass into the wood. This entrance is way marked.

Follow the footpath downwards into a steep gully and a stream at the bottom with a footbridge. Cross this and up some steps passing over a stile into a field. Walking straight across this field bearing slightly right you will see a long hedgerow in the distance. Head towards the gap in this hedgerow, which is in the top right-hand corner of the field. Passing through this gap into the next field go in the direction of a seven-bar metal gate. This leads you into a small farmhouse area where you will bear right and up a small roadway. Immediately by the next gate, turn sharp left into a small field.

(2) Keeping the hedgerow to your right, cross through another gate opposite and into a bridleway with tall hedges either side. Follow this bridleway all the way down into the valley and cross a stream at the bottom by a footbridge. Continue opposite up a hill and through a copse (look out for bluebells in Spring). Pass through a gate into an open field. Keep in the same direction following a wire fence and then a hedge to your right. Pass through another gate and bear right into an enclosed track way.

(3) Carry on along the track way for some distance until you join a main road. Cross over and turn left to double back on the road where to your right is a concreted driveway to "Water Mill Farm" as signposted.

(4) Continue downhill on the driveway to the bottom and cross a bridge. Before you is a farm complex, where you immediately wheel to your right into an open field. Continue through this field keeping the wooded streams to your right. Cross over a turf bridge where you will eventually arrive at an artificial lake. Keep alongside this lake with the stream opposite on your right, when you will arrive at a roadway. Turn right onto this

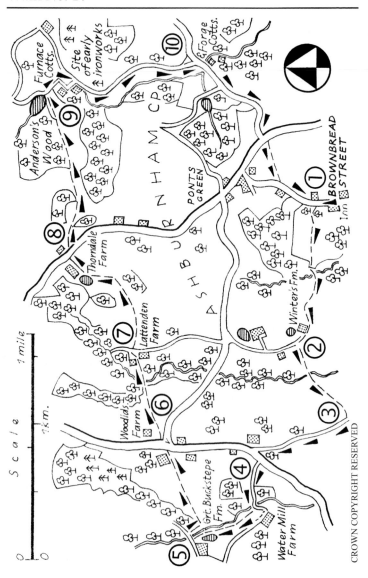

roadway and over a bridge turning immediately right again by the riverbank.

(5) Climb a slope to your left leaving the riverbank to your right, into an open field. Cross directly over this field to the corner of a hedgerow and continue alongside this hedge on your right and eventually through three gates until you arrive at a farm. Passing the farmhouse and barns to your left you will come to a main road again.

Opposite is a handsome large Sussex hall house and barn. A decorative sign fixed on the gable end gives the name of this house "Redpale". Turn left along this road past a junction right and just beyond, turn right into a farm track.

(6) Avoiding the gate on the right, go through the gate ahead, which takes you into a small field. Note to your left in the distance an impressive sight of a high ridge with fields and woods, which is Wood's Corner. Go straight ahead into this field and veer to the left towards a metal gate situated in the middle of a long hedgerow. Pass through this gate, then immediately turn right, then corner left following the hedgerow down hill to the end of the field. Pass through another gate on your right, then over a stile into a steep wooded gully - full of bluebells in spring - towards a twisting stream. Cross over by the

footbridge and up the embankment opposite, over a stile into an open field. Go straight across until you see a large farmhouse and barns ahead. Pass through gates between the farmhouse and barns to your right into the yard curving left. Follow this but turn sharp right at the farm's entrance gates over a stile into a field.

(7) Climb a steep hill alongside and to the right of a hedgerow. At the top there is a stile on the left. Cross this into an open field, going directly towards a wire fence and stile at the right hand corner. Going over this stile continue directly towards a group of trees in the distance surrounding a small pond. Keep to the right of these trees curving left behind them onto a stile. This takes you into another field and by walking towards the barns in the distance you pass through a gate to the right into the farmyard driveway, which takes you onto the main road.

(8) Cross this road towards a stile opposite and pass into a garden enclosure. Walk down this enclosure towards the right and over another stile to the right into a small coppice. Leaving by another stile, go up a steep hill into a field and walk straight ahead to a promontory of trees to the right. Veer left to a gate into an open valley. The path, or track way, inclines towards a forest on your

Walk No. 17

One of the original cottages, Ashburnham Ironworks

left. Ahead are spectacular views of forests in the distance arising on a steep ridge in the general direction of Penhurst.

Continue downhill along this wide track, which eventually follows the right hand perimeter of this forest. Towards the bottom of the hill you reach a wooden gate. Before passing through into the field beyond, stop a moment and have a look about. Ahead you will notice rooftops and dormer windows arising between all the trees. This is the site of the early ironworks, which were operating until the 19th Century. At the bottom of this field, go through a gate on your left.

(9) Immediately turn right on a tree flanked roadway and follow the road right again where you will see a group of early cottages. These are now private residences but were originally built as one of the working buildings, abundant in Sussex for the iron works during the 17th and 18th centuries.

Opposite on your left is evidence of large ponds and structures, which once housed waterpower to operate these machines for the ironworks. Follow the road as it bends to the left down an incline and turns right along a sealed road. This continues for about half a mile until you arrive at a junction with another

Walk No. 17

road rising steeply. Turn right onto this road.

(10) Notice on your left by a waterfall another group of houses well below this road. Some of these were again forge cottages, now privately owned. Opposite to the right of this road are green fields, which would have been artificial lakes.

The remaining section of this walk is clearly signposted as the 1066 Country Walk. Follow the road for about half a mile to a junction. Cross over towards a stile opposite and into some fields. Keeping the hedgerow to your right you will arrive at another roadway. Turn left onto this road when you will eventually arrive at your starting point by the Inn, in Brownbread Street.

Walk No. 18

Brightling Circular, starting at Darwell Hole
5 miles (8 kilometres)

The small village of Brightling is about 13 miles (20 kilometres) north-west of Hastings and is set in the beautiful wooded landscape of the Sussex Weald. It is chiefly known for its eccentric eighteenth century squire, John Fuller, who was responsible for the erection on his estate of several interesting follies which still exist today. This walk will provide the opportunity of seeing some of these and will be an introduction to the lovely local countryside .

Bus services to Brightling are limited and therefore private transport is recommended for this walk. To reach the starting-point take the road from Battle to Heathfield and turn right at Darwell

Hole which is about half a mile beyond Netherfield. Go down the road for about a quarter of a mile and you will find parking on the right at the entrance to Darwell Wood.

(1) From the car park take the broad bridle-way past the metal gate. The path initially goes under a power-line and follows the course of the Darwell Stream through Darwell Wood. After about 600 yards (550 metres) the track forks. Take the right-hand fork and after about 30 yards (27 metres) go left where there is another intersection. Continue along this following the bridle-way sign until the track bends sharply round to the right. Take the signposted path to the

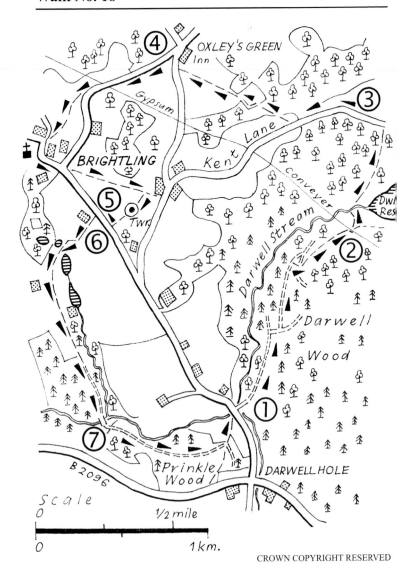

OXLEY'S GREEN
Inn
Gypsum
Kent Lane
Conveyer
BRIGHTLING
Twr.
Darwell Stream
Owl Res
Darwell
Wood
Prinkle Wood
DARWELL HOLE
B 2096

Scale
0
½ mile

0
1 km.

left which leads through coppiced woodland. Go through the wooden gateway into Darwell Reservoir woods and follow the track through the woods until you come to the gypsum mines conveyor-belt. This was built to carry gypsum rock from the mine near Brightling to the processing plant at Mountfield.

(2) Cross the bridge over the conveyor-belt and turn left along the track. After 30 yards (27 metres) take the right-hand fork. Continue and just after the bridge over the stream turn right along the signposted path into the wood. Follow this well-signposted path through the woods which fringe the western end of Darwell Reservoir until you emerge through a small car-park onto a quiet road. Darwell Reservoir was built in the 1950's and is one of the main sources of water for Hastings.

(3) Turn left along this road (Kent Lane) for about 600 yards (550 metres). About 50 yards (45 metres) past the brick bridge, through which the original aerial ropeway went, turn right through a fieldgate into a field. Walk diagonally left downhill almost to the far corner. You will find a stile leading into the woodland. Climb this and bear left through the wood (this can be difficult because of the undergrowth) until you find the bridge which crosses the gully. Above the bridge you will notice

netting which was to protect walkers from possible spillage from the aerial ropeway. It is now almost impossible to cross the gully by the present dilapidated bridge. However it is possible to bypass the bridge and avoid the gully by walking over a culvert about 10 yards (9 metres) to the right. Climb up the bank into the field and follow round the edge to the left until you come to the gap into the next field.

Go forward keeping close to the hedge on your right and proceed through the field towards the buildings ahead. After about 150 yards (135 metres) veer slightly to the left and make for the hedge just to the left of the buildings. About 150 yards (135 metres) to the left of a large building, the "Jack Fullers" inn, you will see an opening in the hedge which will take you out to the road. Turn right along the road to the crossroads (Oxleys Green).

(4) At the crossroads turn left up the road to Brightling and continue for about half a mile (800 metres). About 150 yards (135 metres) after crossing the conveyor-belt bridge climb the stile on your right just before the road bends round to the left. Walk uphill, initially following the hedge on your left, and then the power line until it goes sharply to the left. At this point continue uphill along the hedge on your right to the corner of the field. Climb

John Fuller's Tower

the stile you find there and walk diagonally right across the paddock to the lane in front of the house on the far side. Go right along the lane to the road and left along the road to the entrance gate of Brightling Church. A visit to the church is well worthwhile. On the left as you enter the churchyard you will see the pyramid under which squire John Fuller is buried. John Fuller died in 1834 but had arranged for the pyramid to be built in 1810, twenty four years before his demise. The church stands on high ground adjacent to Brightling Park. It is built of local sandstone and has a lovely mellow colour in keeping

with the local area. It dates back to sometime after 1066.

To continue the walk proceed down the road from the churchyard entrance until you reach a road junction. Immediately opposite you will see a kissing gate. Go through and follow the fence on your left-hand side. Pause as you walk down this path and admire the fine views to the north and east. At the next fence go through the kissing gate and continue straight on to the hedge ahead. Go through the kissing gate you find here and follow the path with the hedge on your left to another kissing gate.

Walk No. 18

Go through and turn immediately right, climbing over a stile, and walk alongside the hedge. Enter a copse straight ahead by means of a stile or gate on your right to reach the Tower.

(5) The Tower is another of John Fuller's follies. It is 35 feet (10.7 metres) high and was built, it is said, so that he could see Bodiam Castle, which he purchased in 1828 to save it from demolition by builders. Although the Tower has been repaired in recent years and an iron staircase installed, it is currently thought to be unsafe and the public warned against climbing it.

Leave the Tower and continue walking in the same direction by the path on the western side and walk down across the field to the road. If you pause on your way down and look ahead to the south-west you will be able to see the temple in the middle of the park and on the far horizon the "Sugar Loaf", two more of Fuller's follies. The latter was built, it is said, as a result of a wager he had with a friend that he could see Dallington Church from his house. When he found he could not see the church he had the Sugar Loaf built to mimic a church spire and enable him to win the wager.

(6) Turn right along the road for about 60 yards (55 metres) and then left through the gateway into the estate. Notice the stone boundary wall as you pass into the estate. John Fuller had this built to give work to the unemployed. It is four miles (6.5 kilometres) long and was constructed mainly between 1815 and 1817.

Follow the broad track as it curves downhill gently to the right then swings sharply to the left. After 500 yards (450 metres) you will pass farm buildings on your right-hand side. Continue in the same direction and when you reach a fork ignore the track to the left and follow the bridleway which carries straight on with the wood on the left. Carry on downhill with trees now on both sides and ignore tracks to the left and right.

(7) Eventually you will reach a bridge over a stream. Cross this and continue along the track past the cottage on the left and follow it as it bears gently to the left. It continues its way through Prinkle Wood, initially with broad-leaved trees and later conifers on either side. At a junction of paths continue straight on following the signposted route. As the land drops away to the left there are good views across to Cackle Street and Twelve Oaks. Shortly after this the track bears left quite sharply and goes down to the road. Opposite is your starting point at Darwell Hole.

Walk No. 19

Burwash, Batemans and the Upper Dudwell Valley
7½ miles (12 kilometres)

Bateman's, Burwash

(A hilly walk with glorious views, muddy paths in wet weather) Burwash is an attractive place with old houses and buildings along a ridge between the valley of the rivers Rother to the north and Dudwell to the south. There is a fine church and some pleasant pubs where meals can be had, as well as a tearoom for refreshments. Burwash was at one time a centre of the Sussex Iron Industry and many of the fine buildings, including Socknersh Manor and Batemans, were at one time houses belonging to ironmasters.

(1) From the public car park by the Bear take the path in the southeast corner by the Scout Hut. Follow the path down the field to a stile in the hedge on the right. Follow this path with a fence on your right to a stile in the corner, immediately cross a plank bridge and another stile and then continue along the path with the hedge on the right and after approx. 150 yards (136 metres) cross the stile on the right. Go half left across the next field to a stile in the bottom right hand corner and to a further stile at the bottom of the field, out on to the road.

(2) Turn right to approach Batemans after about 200 yards (182 metres). Batemans was originally an Ironmasters house and the date over the entrance porch is shown as 1634. Following the decline of the iron industry in Sussex, these large houses suffered neglect and fell into disuse or became farm houses. Rudyard Kipling bought Batemans in 1902 and this remained his home until his death in 1936. It afforded him greater privacy and isolation than his previous house at Rottingdean. On the death of his wife in 1939 the house was bequeathed to the National Trust as a memorial to the poet and author. Facing Batemans take the road on the left, which soon goes past some cottages.

(3) At Corner Cottage turn right and take the path round the reservoir for Batemans Mill and continue along the path into the woods. After about 90 yards (82 metres), turn right over a bridge and continue in the same direction across a field. In the far right hand corner go right over a stile, turn immediately left to next stile, cross this and follow the track between hedges until a tarmac road is reached. Bear immediately left past the farmhouse, Rye Green Farm, cross stile and proceed half right across field and through a copse to next stile. Continue across field to top left hand corner and cross stile. Keep hedge on your

right go through a field gate and two kissing gates and turn right to next field gate.

(4) Go past Pear Tree Cottage and continue up a lane past Burnt House Farm and out on to the main road (A265). On reaching the road cross to pavement and turn left, after 400 yards you reach the Wheel Inn.

(5) At the Wheel Inn, go down Willingford Lane opposite for about 20 yards (18 metres) and turn right on to the footpath. Follow this path, which descends quite steeply through a wood. At the bottom cross a stile and go across the footbridge. The path then climbs steeply. Maintain a southerly direction with a fence on your left. At the top of the wood, cross a stile into a field and continue in the same direction to a stile and out on to a lane. Turn left past some farm buildings and continue past Henhurst Farm (formerly Parkhill Farm) (6) in the same direction, on a path and then a track through a wood.

Cross a stile into a field, maintaining same direction (ignore stile on the right) and continue to a stile at the end of the field in the right hand corner. Maintain direction across next field and pass through a gap in the hedge into a further field. Proceed to far side and cross a bridge over a stream. Follow the line of trees ahead and then bear

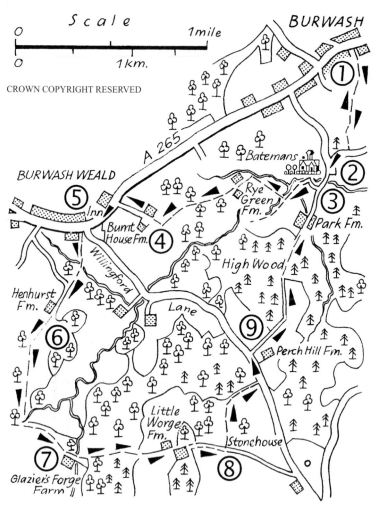

half right to a gap in the hedge. From this point follow the contour towards some farm buildings and on reaching these cross a stile on the right and then straight on to Glaziers Forge Farm.

Walk No. 19

(7) Turn left along the track and after 150 yards (136 metres) pass wooden garage and take the bridleway on the left up through the woods. Follow this track, ignoring crossing paths, to Little Worge Farm. Continue past the converted farm buildings along a concrete track. After about half a mile (800 metres), ignore the first footpath on the left and proceed towards a house (Stonehouse).

(8) Just before the house, take the footpath on the left. Go through the gate (or over if locked) through a second gate and down through a gap in a line of trees. Continue to the far right corner, initially keeping to the right of the hedge, cross the stile and with the wood on the left continue to a further stile and out on to the road (Willingford Lane) Turn left along this road until you reach Perch Hill Farm.

(9) A hundred yards (91 metres) past the farm take the bridleway on the right. On reaching a house along this track, join a footpath continuing in the same direction. Follow this down through a wood, crossing a forest road, and continue along the signposted bridleway opposite. Go through a gate and down the left hand side of a field to a path which enters the wood. Follow the path down through a farm (Park Farm) and out on to a lane which leads back to Batemans. Return to Burwash from here by retracing the original route.

Squeeze Gate, near Burwash

Walk No. 20

Stonegate Station Circular including Burwash
7¼ or 8¼ miles (11.6 or 13.2 kilometres)

*Burwash

This walk explores the beautiful Sussex Weald and has fine views across the countryside . There were once several iron working sites in the area, some dating from Roman times.

The route is about 7¼ miles (11.6 kilometres) , but can be increased by around another mile to include a visit to Burwash, where there are refreshment facilities. Stonegate village is centred on a cross-roads about 2½ miles (4 kilometres) north of Burwash village and 20 miles (32 kilometres) north-west of Hastings. The road running NE to

SW at the cross-roads is of Roman origin. To the south-west is the Parish Church and further on is the railway station.

The church, built of red brick, dates from 1904, replacing an earlier church of 1838. The station is of South Eastern Railway origin and was built for the opening of the railway in 1851, when it was named Witherenden, subsequently Ticehurst Road until 1947, when it became Stonegate.

There is a good rail service between Hastings and Tunbridge Wells.

Walk No. 20

The walk starts at the station (National Grid Ref. TQ659272). Leave the car park by way of the farm drive opposite the station building and pass a second car park on the left. At the top turn right in front of a house, keeping a pond on the right. Follow the track for a few yards to the end of the house garden where there is a waymarked track to the left. Turn left up this farm track to where there is a pond in the field on the left. **(1)** Opposite is a waymarked gate and stile into a field. Head across this field at an angle making for the left hand end of a row of trees, in which there is a pond, in line with a converted barn on the left of the field near a house. Pass through the gateway and follow the footpath to just above the opposite corner of this field. Near here was once an early ironworks. On the way Burwash church and Brightling Needle (a stone column) can be seen to the right. Cross the stile and enter a copse. The footpath is well defined and follows a stream (on its right) before crossing it and climbing steeply up to a field. Turn left and walk up the field, keeping to the left hand hedge and wood. Pass through the gap ahead into the next field, still keeping the wood on the left. After about 90 yards (80 metres) cross the stile on the left, thus re-entering the wood. Turn sharp right and follow the right hand hedge to emerge into a field over a stile.

Walk up this field - keeping alongside wood on the left - to a stile and farm gate **(3)**. Do *not* cross into the next field, but turn sharp right and walk alongside the hedge (now on one's left) to a stile in a corner. Once in the next field proceed with hedge on the left until near a corner where the footpath veers slightly to the right, to pass through a copse by way of a broad path with a pond on the right. Once in the next field follow the left hand hedge, passing a pond on the left, and later a clump of trees with another pond in an adjacent field. Continue alongside the hedge and pass through an opening into another field. Again keeping hedge on the left, proceed almost to the corner but veer a little to the right to an opening in the hedge where there are the remains of a stile. On entering the next field keep to the left hand hedge, but where it turns away to the left keep straight ahead to a concrete driveway, on the way crossing a weir with a pond on the left. Turn left up the driveway and follow it to join a road. Notice the array of farm machinery in the garden on the left.

Turn left along this road for about 250 yards (227 metres), passing Bearhurst Farm on the left, to where the road makes a left hand bend. Here on the right is a terrace of houses, before which there is a footpath and farm gate **(5)**.

STONEGATE

Stonegate Rly. Sta.

Old Shoyswell Manor Farm

Martlets

Witherenden Bridge

Eatonden Mnr. Fm.

River Rother

Wreckery Bridge

Franchise Manor

Mottynsden Mnr. Hs.

Mottynsden Farm

Dawes Fm.

BURWASH

Scale

0   1 mile

0   1 km.

Walk No. 20

Turn right along the footpath alongside the first house named "Clayball Cottage" into a field, then straight ahead to a stile. After crossing the stile the footpath veers away from the left hand hedge - where there is a deep hollow - and, still keeping almost in line with the previous footpath, drop into a valley heading for a gap in the hedge to the right of a metal cattle trough. Cross a stile beside a farm gate and walk up the field ahead keeping to the right hand hedge. Cross another stile close to a cattle trough. Once in next field walk straight ahead to a gap in the trees to find a five bar gate **(6)**. Turn right and admire the view, then walk alongside a wood. Where the wood ends continue in the same direction down to the bottom left-hand corner of the field to find an iron five bar gate leading on to a farm track. Turn left along this track passing farm buildings on each side and continue into hollow where Old Shoyswell Manor can be seen on the right **(7)**. Follow the drive from the Manor a short distance to the end of the conifer hedge. Before the drive turns sharp left, take the first signposted track to the right down past a cottage (on left) to a stile and a gate. Turn left alongside a stream to a gate and stile overhung by trees.

From here walk up the field, passing under power cables, to the fence at the right hand side of a large clump of trees to find a stile and farm gate. Cross the stile and follow direction indicated by waymark on top of post, then continue alongside the trees to a stile, and ahead to another stile onto a concrete driveway where there is a signposted cross-roads of Rights-of-Way. **(8)**

Turn right along the concrete drive to join Battenhurst road. Walk straight ahead passing the drive to two dwellings on the right to where the road dips and turns right. On the left in the dip is the entrance to Eatonden Manor Farm. Turn left along the concrete farm driveway. In front of a gate leading to the farmhouse there is a wide fenced track - signposted - to the right. Follow the track to where it turns sharp left into a farmyard. On the bend cross a stile on the right and head to a farm gate and stile in the far left corner of the field. When in the next field head for the far right hand corner to a gate and stile. Turn left immediately after crossing the stile to cross another stile into a field. Keep alongside hedge to another stile and iron gate leading into a wooded area **(9)**. Follow the well defined footpath through the wood until confronted by a wire fence. Turn left for 130 yards (118 metres), then right over a stile and continue along this meandering footpath (which can be muddy)

Walk No. 20

to emerge into a field. Head down the field to the bottom left-hand corner alongside the railway-line embankment. Keeping the railway line on the left, cross a stream and follow the left hand hedge and conifer trees to find a stile leading to the railway line by way of a gate **(10)**. Beware of trains! Cross the railway and pass through a gate into a field. Follow the waymarked route across the field to the end of a hedge, then bearing left head for a bridge across a stream. Continue to the right of a clump of trees **(11)** and follow alongside to a marker post and then a second marker post. Here, turn right to Wreckery Bridge. After crossing the bridge, head for the far left corner of the field to find a stile and gate on the left, and a signpost **(12)**.

At this point there is the option of diverting to Burwash for the longer walk. In which case turn left over the stile and then sharp right alongside the hedge and stream to the far right corner of the field. Pass through gate and bear half left as waymarked to stile into a wood. Follow the wandering footpath up to a stile into a field. The footpath then veers away from the left hand fence and heads up to the right of two large old trees. Continue to the top of the field and through a gate on to the farm drive **(13)**. Follow this drive to the right until it joins Burwash High Street. (For

notes on Burwash see walk no.19) Turn right along High Street to the Catholic Church, and take the driveway beyond to Dawes Farm. Keeping the farmhouse, with its truncated Oast, on the left, **(14)** cross a stile/farmgate to enter a field. Follow the line of trees on the right through this, and a second field, to arrive at a footbridge. Cross the bridge and turn sharp left down to a farm gate. Through the gate and on to another gate in the valley bottom where there is a stream. Walk up next field keeping to the right and pass through an iron gate to join a private drive. On the left is Mottynsden Farm **(15)**. Keeping right, walk along the drive to Mottynsden House. Just before the house take the path to the left up to an orchard. Turn right, keeping hedge on right, to join the road at a cross-roads of rights-of-way. **(16)** Here the route picks up that taken by the shorter walk.

Those taking the shorter walk should turn right at the signpost where the walks diverged **(12)**. Follow the left hand hedge through two fields up to a stile leading to a third field heading, as waymarked, to a stile almost at the top right corner. Across the field Franchise Manor can be seen to the right. Once over the stile turn left up the drive for about 140 yards (127 metres) to arrive at the cross-roads of Rights-of-Way, thus joining the

(16)

Walk No. 20

route from Burwash. Turn into the field where there is a waymarked footpath to the left of a paddock. Follow the footpath with wire fence on right to the end of some cottages. Cross over two stiles in quick succession, then across a garden to a third stile to enter a field. Continue, with wire fence on right, to a farmgate and stile **(17)** A large pond can be seen to the right. Over the stile strike across the field heading for a footbridge to the left of the apex of the field. A white gabled house on the hill beyond is a guide to the direction to take.

Over the footbridge walk straight ahead to the corner of a tall hedge, and by way of a gap enter a hop field. Follow the left boundary of the hop field to its end and then turn half right in the next field to a farm gate. Once through this gate turn half left to another farmgate leading on to a road **(18)**. Turn right along the road to Witherenden Bridge dating from 1790; to the left, upstream once stood a watermill. Continue on the road to the house named Martlets **(19)** on the right. Immediately beyond the house is a waymarked bridleway. Pass through three gates along the bridleway. Then climb the path up a field to an iron bridlegate in a wire mesh fence, ignoring a track curving to the right. Cross the railway bridge into a field. The route ahead skirts farmbuildings and a pond on the left then winds round to a farm gate on to a driveway near some houses **(20)**. Turn left and follow the path between the pond and the house back to the railway station.